The Appearance of Bridges and Other Highway Structures

The Appearance of Bridges and Other Highway Structures

 THE HIGHWAYS AGENCY

London: HMSO

THE HIGHWAYS AGENCY

 THE SCOTTISH OFFICE INDUSTRY DEPARTMENT

 **THE WELSH OFFICE
Y SWYDDFA GYMREIG**

 **THE DEPARTMENT OF THE ENVIRONMENT
FOR NORTHERN IRELAND**

ISBN 0 11 551804 5

There are few features, whether of countryside or town, which attract more notice than bridges. Some illustrate the fitting use of local materials by our forefathers, while others provide pleasing examples of modern design. In recent years the increase in traffic has impelled highway authorities to undertake the strengthening of many ancient and new bridges and the building of many additional structures.

It is possible for a bridge to comply with structural standards and yet the bridge and its approaches to fall short of the legitimate expectations of the public in the matter of architectural design and suitability to its surroundings.

As the Minister responsible for many bridges I wish to impress upon all authorities the great importance of securing at the outset the best expert advice upon the design – not merely from the standpoint of the stability and safety of the structure, but also of its proportions and appearance.

This advice follows very closely the advice on aesthetics given in 1925 by the then Minister of Transport to road authorities on the importance of the appearance of bridges. The technology may well have changed, but the principles of good design and sensitivity to the environment remain the same, so the advice is just as valid today. The appearance of roads and their structures is important to all people in the UK, whether observing on foot or from a vehicle.

The vast majority of bridges are built at public expense. Whether it is a major motorway bridge over a river estuary, or a pedestrian bridge connecting a footpath in the remote uplands, we should expect the best possible design for its context. This publication confirms the Government's concern for good design in the environment, and tries to educate and inspire both engineers and clients to seek beautiful bridges.

The principles it sets out should set a benchmark for design quality for structures associated with roads, which include retaining walls, tunnels, and ancillary buildings as well as bridges. The illustrations show the variety of possible design solutions, and the excellence it has been possible to achieve both in the UK and abroad. But the illustrations are not exhaustive, there is enormous scope yet for further new designs.

I commend this publication to all those designing or commissioning roads.

John Watts
Minister for Railways and Roads

Contents   **The Appearance of Bridges and Other Highway Structures**

Chapter 1
Introduction and principles

1.1 BACKGROUND
The Department of Transport (DoT) has been promoting high aesthetic standards in bridge design since 1925, when the then Minister circulated a note on the subject to road authorities. The first edition of *The Appearance of Bridges*, published in 1964, was based on that advice, and the present book forms an updating and expansion. However, it goes into more depth and covers a wider field, reflecting the shift in emphasis on response to the environment, changing construction techniques, and changing approaches to design. It is intended to be read in conjunction with Advice Note BA 41/94, 'The Design and Appearance of Bridges', which gives guidelines on the basic principles of design as well as the scope of work expected from those designing bridges.

1.2 PURPOSE OF THE BOOK
This guide is not intended to be prescriptive, but to help ensure that all aspects of visual excellence are considered and achieved, irrespective of design philosophy. The last thing UK trunk road authorities or the Royal Fine Art Commissions (RFAC and RFACS) want is a set of standard solutions or the automatic application of any particular formula. To quote the RFAC, 'use the guidelines as a check list rather than a straitjacket'.* Variety is vital: not only that variety which comes from differing local character and tradition, but also that rarer sort which is to be found in occasional brilliant departure from the orthodox. Britain boasts as fine a tradition in bridge building as any in the world, and it would be a matter for regret if anything said here tended to sap the sources of this originality. Men like John Rennie, Thomas Telford and IK Brunel enjoyed international reputations, and their works are a source of continual admiration. Why should not our own generation, for all its differences in taste and technique, make as notable a contribution?

1.3 USE OF THE BOOK
This book is intended to be used by:
(a) engineers designing bridges
(b) architects consulted by bridge engineers on aesthetics
(c) landscape architects who wish to understand the philosophy of bridge design in relation to their designs
(d) planning authorities and members of the public who have an interest in the appearance of bridges.

1.4 ARRANGEMENT OF THE BOOK
The chapters are arranged in a way that attempts to separate considerations arising out of the various structural forms *per se* from those pertaining to bridge function, as well as matters relevant to all bridges, and other special circumstances.

1.2a (left) OLD WATERLOO BRIDGE, London.

1.2b (below) CRAIGELLACHIE BRIDGE, River Spey, Scotland.

1.2c (below) CLIFTON SUSPENSION BRIDGE, Bristol.

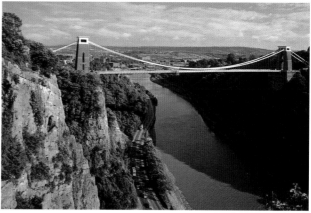

* From *Planning for Beauty*, HMSO 1990.

1.6a (right) ALAMILLO BRIDGE, Seville. One function of this bridge was to be a symbol of Seville Expo '92.

1.7a (above) BRAY VIADUCT, Devon. The individual character is provided by re-used masonry piers.

1.8a (left) SALGINATOBEL BRIDGE, near Schiers, Switzerland: unity of form and detail.

Basic principles are highlighted in *italics*, e.g. *The guidance given in this book is to improve the appearance of bridges and other structures associated with roads.*

Illustrations relate to particular paragraphs and share the same number; e.g. Figs. 3.3a and 3.3b illustrate Chapter 3, Paragraph 3 (**3.3**). Where the information was available, designer (**d**) and photographer (**ph**) are given at the end of each chapter. They are not intended in every case to represent ideal designs, and in some cases do no more than amplify some specific point in the text. Some demonstrate particularly bad examples. Others, however, are intended to show alternative solutions to familiar problems and to inspire new designs.

1.5 EXPRESSION OF FUNCTION
It is generally accepted that expression of function is the basis of good design, and that any adjustment or addition required to improve the appearance should exploit this functional basis and not run counter to it. FORM, CHARACTER, DETAIL, SCALE and PROPORTION are the five aspects of design which have to be considered from first principles. They are closely interrelated and all the advice in this book relates back to these principles. They are just as valid no matter what approach or philosophy of design the engineer or architect believes in.

1.6 FORM
Form derives from a balance of functions in the broadest sense. These may be the load to be carried, structural needs, navigational clearances, construction difficulties or environmental needs. In exceptional circumstances the function can even be as a monument or symbol.

1.7 CHARACTER
Character and individuality are no less important. *A bridge should not only be attractive to look at, and express the sense of achievement, however modest, inherent in all well-designed bridges; it should have in addition a natural and permanent association with its setting.*

1.8 DETAIL
The quantity and quality of expressed detail are critical to the scale, proportion and perceived attention to beauty of a bridge. The closer you look at something natural, the more detail you will see, and the best design seeks to emulate this. Visual texture and structural patterns repeat at different scales, as in the branches of a tree and the veins of a leaf, and this unity of form and detail can be utilized in bridges, e.g. the arch form of the Salginatobel Bridge and its deck scuppers. The purpose of

1.8b (right) Kingsgate Footbridge, River Wear, Durham: expression of important constructional detail.

1.8c (far right) Olgastrasse Footbridge, Zürich, Switzerland: complex structure clearly expressed.

1.9a (below) Vauxhall Cross, London. Both the ground floor and the river wall are 12m high concrete walls, but appear small-scale.

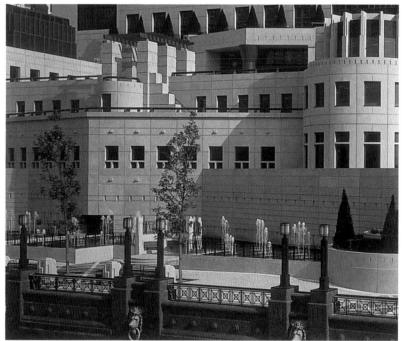

1.9b (above) Gade Valley Viaduct, Hertfordshire: a large and oppressive 12m high concrete leaf pier.

good quality detailing is to express function, making it clear what you are apparently seeing – and it is usually best to express the truth. If it is a railway bridge, do not make it match the road bridges; if it is a pinned arch, express the pin joints; if it is a stone arch, express the voussoirs; if it has plastic cladding, express it as cladding. When the structure is unusual, it is particularly important to express how it works in its detail.

1.9 | **Scale**
Scale is whether something appears to be large and oppressive or small and intimate, but it is relative, not absolute. The same object, e.g. a 12m high concrete wall, can appear large-scale or small-scale depending on the detailed design. Designers should

be conscious of which they want to achieve and not leave it to accident. The wrong scale can be inappropriate, look foolish or oppressive, and stir up heated objections. Perception of scale is dependent on two things: the size of a person relative to everything else, and the effect of light. To quote Protagoras (via Plato and the Prince of Wales), 'Man is the measure of all things'.

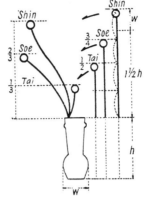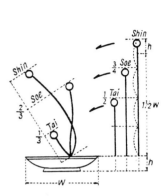

1.10b (below) Japanese Flower Arranging (Ikebana): one of the few proportional systems for asymmetry.

1.10a (above) The Five Orders of Architecture: the most well-known proportional system.

proportions are recognized they appear right and therefore beautiful; when there is no mathematical relationship the design looks awkward. Where the inherent proportions are greater than 1:7, e.g. deck depth to span, or deck clearance to span on long-span bridges, a modulation of the long dimension, e.g. with constructional joints or suspension hangers, helps with proportions. It should also be remembered that proportions are seen in three dimensions.

1.11 ENVIRONMENTAL INTRUSION
One further principle is relevant to the non-bridge items also covered in this document. Generally the intrusion of roads upon the environment should be minimized. *Therefore all structures not directly part of the road should harmonize with the adjacent environment and context rather than merely relate to the road itself.* This applies to retaining walls, landscaping, service buildings and yards, environmental barriers, motorway service areas, culverts, rock fences, balancing ponds, etc., as well as to footbridges and equestrian bridges over features like water courses, which are built to divert such routes because of the construction of a new road.

PICTURE CREDITS
1.2a d John Rennie. **1.2b d** Thomas Telford. **1.2c d** IK Brunel; ph E Nagele. **1.6a d** Santiago Calatrava; ph John Linden. **1.7a d** ph Gifford Graham & Partners. **1.8a d** Robert Maillart; ph JW (Jon Wallsgrove, as throughout volume). **1.8b d** Ove Arup; ph JW. **1.8c d** Santiago Calatrava; ph JW. **1.9a d** Terry Farrell; ph Jo Reid/ John Peck. **1.9b d** Frederick Gibberd & Partners. **1.10a d** Vignola. **1.10b d** Ikenobo Senei.

1.10 PROPORTION
Proportion is the relationship of the parts to each other and to the whole. For the purpose of this document it can be distilled down into the desirability of keeping the major dimensions of a bridge in a simple mathematical relationship of whole numbers less than 7. It has been said that 7 is the maximum number the brain can recognize without counting, so ratios – as of a span to height – are recognized without conscious thought when the largest number is 7 – e.g. 1:7, 2:3, 1:2:4. When the

Chapter 2

Context and setting of bridges

2.1 *The horizontal and vertical alignment of a bridge relative to its topographical context has more effect on the bridge's appearance than any other single factor.*

2.2 Usually the position of a bridge in its setting is largely determined when routes are being considered. The following factors should therefore be addressed at the earliest stages, since to achieve beautiful bridges, especially on schemes where bridges are a dominant factor, should be one of the influences on route selection.

2.3 *The first step is to decide whether the bridge in its setting should be low-key or a bold statement.* The decision is helped by carrying out a visual appraisal of the landscape. If the topography is dramatic or the setting mundane or mutilated, a bold statement is frequently appropriate. If the structure is long or high or has a large individual span, it will inevitably be bold, so the boldness should be celebrated and made more dramatic. If the topography or scenery is gentle or beautiful, it can usually take a dramatic bridge less easily. If a location already has striking features close by, especially important bridges or buildings, again a more low-key approach is usually appropriate, as is also the case where a new bridge intrudes on a familiar 'picture postcard' view and cannot be avoided. Where bridges are frequent, as with overbridges on a motorway, they should generally be low-key to make them less noticeable, but the opportunity should be taken every so often to exploit minor drama in the topography or functional needs to make a bold statement to enliven journeys, and enhance driver alertness and awareness of location.

2.4 The drama of a bridge and usually the general appearance are enhanced by great height – and height is emphasized when length is reduced. Therefore it is better to have a high short crossing than a longer lower one.

2.5 Bridge abutments tend to be visually improved if they come out of a natural steep slope, and the steeper the better. Visually, shear rock faces are excellent.

2.3a (right) KINGSGATE FOOTBRIDGE, River Wear, Durham: dramatic setting.

2.3b (below) JAPAN BRIDGE, La Défense, Paris: mundane setting made dramatic by the bridge.

2.5a (left) PONT DE TANCARVILLE, Le Havre, Normandy, France. Springing from the rock face looks better than an approach viaduct.

2.8a (right) M40 Bridge, High Wycombe. Planting improves abutments.

2.8b (centre) A1 Bridge, Wentbridge, West Yorkshire. Planted wood here visually narrows the valley.

2.9a (bottom) A27 Bridge, River Adur, Shoreham-by-Sea, West Sussex. Bridge links ridge across skyline notch.

2.5b (below) Navajo Bridge, Arizona. Rock faces make visually excellent abutments.

2.6 The best level for an abutment, where the site permits, is at a natural change in slope from a steep hillside to the more gentle incline of a plateau. This is usually determined by the specific geology at the bridge; where there is a rock cutting, variations in strata may require this change in angle of slope for structural reasons – and this should be exploited.

2.7 Where there is the possibility of using an old quarry for a bridge location this should be taken, since it enhances the drama of the bridge, often reduces visibility from a distance, and gives an opportunity to improve the landscape of the immediate area.

2.8 Bridges often look better if abutments are deliberately masked within woodland. The road should be located through woodland where it is extensive and planted, or along one edge with new planting on the other side of the road where the woodland is small, ancient or open to the public. Trees on the natural hillside below and beside a bridge abutment mask any retaining walls at the abutment and can help the proportions by visually narrowing a narrow valley, and thus enhancing the height-to-span ratio.

2.9 Where a road cuts through a ridge, and an overbridge is required which will be seen against the skyline, its deck should follow the skyline slope of the land to visually link

across the skyline notch. The notch should be kept as narrow as possible to enhance the bridge and impinge less on the environment. In this situation a single arch span often works well.

2.10 Footpaths and ancient routes, especially Roman roads, should cross new roads, particularly those in cutting, on the exact old alignment. Where bridges are being rebuilt due to road widening, the opportunity should be taken to reinstate on the ancient line if this has been moved in the past. This includes using a skew crossing where appropriate. The purpose is to render the new bridge much less conspicuous to the user of the path or Roman road. Diverting footpaths alongside new roads to another accommodation structure should be avoided, since the approach to the bridge, and thus appreciation of it, is spoilt for the pedestrians. It is better to divert farm access to the footpath route where practicable, or divert the footpath at some distance from the road.

2.11 Pedestrian bridges should be located using natural contours to avoid ramps on the structure. This is generally preferable to retaining the footpath line where the level is changed in any case.

2.12 River bridges should be positioned to avoid moving the natural curve of the river.

2.13 Long, low viaducts should be positioned to utilize existing clumps of trees, hedges and land form to mask the ends of the viaduct from important views, so as to minimize the apparent length and proximity of the structure. Off-site planting should also be considered, where appropriate.

2.14 Where well-wooded railway embankments or similar features are used as the line for a new road, the new structure and/or embankment should be to one side, so as to utilize the existing planting to eliminate the impact of the new structure and road, at least from one side.

2.15 Broad viaducts and underbridges are very often unpleasant and ugly for those passing under them. Extra breadth is needed for sightlines on tight horizontal curvature. If the road is already broad, e.g. dual three-lane and above, tight horizontal curvatures should be avoided on structures. If the minor road can pass over the major road, a broad underbridge is avoided, which is preferable.

2.16 The high parapets needed for equestrian bridges and for environmental barriers are inevitably ugly, so their use should be avoided by positioning the structure away from residential properties and combining equestrian overbridges with road overbridges, where possible.

2.17 Where bridges and viaducts can be masked by existing trees and woodland or industrial buildings, the vertical alignment should be lowered to keep the structure, and preferably the vehicles, below the treetops or roofline.

2.18 Lighting and signs are needed on approaches to traffic junctions but spoil the simple lines and flow of a bridge when they are placed on it. At the planning stage it is best to keep junctions as far as possible from the end of structures. Similarly, junctions close to bridges often require wing walls and parapets at abutments to curve or angle away from the line of the bridge for sightlines. This can make abutments visually and physically awkward. The problem can be overcome by moving the junction further away or by having both ends treated similarly to give symmetry, which is often a solution at roundabout and dumb-bell grade-separated junctions.

2.19 Where the vertical alignment requires a fall along a bridge, it is usually best to have either a dramatic slope, for bold asymmetry, or an inconspicuous minimal fall (which may avoid drain sumps showing or having to be hidden, by reducing edge cantilevers to a minimum).

2.20 Sag curves and hog-curves on long-span bridges can lead to particular forms of structure being visually more appropriate, e.g. cable-stayed bridges with hog-curves can look as if they are collapsing if they have a central mast. Therefore, where there is scope for adjusting the vertical alignment, this should be done in conjunction with the selection of bridge structure.

2.20a (below) Basin Footbridge, Le Havre, Normandy. Cable-stayed bridge with a hog curve benefits visually by having an asymmetric mast.

2.19a (above) M6 Bridge, Lancashire: bold asymmetry, though a little too heavy.

2.21a (above, left) Avon Bridges, M40, Warwick: carriageways separated because of different bridge types.

2.22a (above) Fowey Bridge, Lostwithiel Bypass, Cornwall. Form of bridge is dictated by materials appropriate to site.

AESTHETIC CHECKLIST

Context

- Natural landscape and topography
- Man-made landscape: existing structures
- History and tradition
- Contemporary intellectual climate and state of development of technology
- Visibility

Form

Visual expression of efficiency
- Slenderness
- Transparency through openings
- Mass

Order and unity
- Organization of structural system
- Coherent cross-sectional shapes

Artistic shaping
- Visual expression of flow of forces
- Cross-sections that minimize stresses
- Light and shadow effects
- Structural and non-structural ornamentation

Detail
o
- Materials
- Finishes
- Detailing
- Scale
- Speed and position of viewers.

2.23a (left) Aesthetic Checklist

2.21 Where a new bridge is adjacent to an existing, it should be parallel and on an identical vertical alignment, but where this is impossible the difference should be contrasted. Unless the structures are identical, the bridges should have as large a gap as possible between them. Where there is a difference in vertical curvature as well as level, the separation should be the greatest to avoid reading the two structures together. In this case the bridges can be non-parallel to help the contrast between structures. Where a new bridge is in line with the existing, such as an overbridge to a new road parallel to a railway, enough space should be left between for them to read separately or to have a prominent abutment between them. These separations need to be considered at the earliest stage since they will affect the alignment on the bridge approach for some distance.

2.22 Where the context of a site dictates certain materials for aesthetic reasons, e.g. stone in a particular national park, and where this context and material dictate certain bridge forms, like a true stone arch, which require particular span and height geometries, this should be taken into account in the vertical and horizontal alignment, and the crossing point.

2.23 There are three stages of design when aesthetics ought to be considered:
- Route planning – which determines CONTEXT
- Concept design – which determines FORM
- Detail design – which determines DETAIL.
The designer, and anyone reviewing a design, should use Fig. 2.23a to ensure that all aspects have been considered.

PICTURE CREDITS
2.3a d Ove Arup; ph JW. **2.3b d** Peter Rice/RFR/Arup; ph JW. **2.5a** ph JW. **2.5b d** RA Hanson; ph JW. **2.8a** ph JW. **2.8b** ph JW. **2.9a** ph JW. **2.19a** ph JW. **2.20a** ph JW. **2.21a d** Arup; ph JW. **2.22a** ph JW.

Chapter 3
Masonry arches

3.1 The masonry arch can be aesthetically desirable in certain settings, for example where a bridge impinges on an old city wall or other solid masonry structure. Many very beautiful arch bridges have been built from the time of the Romans onwards, and new research favours their revival.

3.2 Whereas arch bridges were often enhanced in the past by specifically dressed stone courses, quoins and other features, it is seldom desirable or practicable to attempt such elaboration today. Simple string courses and copings are usually sufficient; any further elaboration demands a high standard of design and craftsmanship if it is to achieve a satisfactory appearance.

3.3 Stone arch bridges have been a standard form of bridge construction since ancient times, and there are many such 2000-year-old bridges still standing and in use. This fact should be borne in mind when the requirement for a 120-year life on a bridge is considered. Hardly any steel and no reinforced concrete bridges have yet stood for 120 years,

and granite is claimed to have better resistance to abrasion from water-borne sand than does concrete.

Recent developments in accurate computer cutting of stone combined with stainless steel ties for tension components may hold potential for the future.

3.4 *A load-bearing masonry arch is preferable to a clad concrete or steel arch, since it is more honest to its material and function.*

3.5 Semicircular, pointed, four- and three-centre, elliptical and parabolic arches are all suitable, and are variously appropriate depending on height, span and clearances required. During the last century IK Brunel adopted the semi-elliptical arch for many of his structures, with notable success aesthetically.

3.6 *Since a new masonry arch is rare, though becoming more common, usually for important environmental reasons, the fact that it is of stone or brick should be expressed and celebrated.*

3.7 Voussoirs are the principal structural element, so should generally be expressed as radiating from the arch centres. Care should be taken if the voussoirs are expressed as a ring, so as to avoid visual confusion with a faced concrete ring arch.

3.3a (above, left) Thames Footbridge, Bloomers Hole, Buscot, Gloucestershire: proposed design using stone and stainless steel.

3.5a (above) Maidenhead Railway Bridge, Berkshire: elegant and huge brick arch.

3.7a (left) Maidenhead Bridge, Berkshire: voussoirs boldly expressed.

3.10a (right) STRASBOURG BRIDGE: simple arch expressing thrust at river banks.

3.8a (below) PONT NOTRE-DAME, Paris. The stone dressing varies correctly with the type of stone.

3.11b (left) OVER BRIDGE: detail of three-dimensional stones.

3.11a (left) OVER BRIDGE, Gloucester: excellent three-dimensional geometry.

3.8 The dressing of the stone is important and should be sensitive to the material's nature. It should be an appropriate finish for modern stone masonry techniques such as laser cutting, diamond sawing, flame texturing and sandblasting. Traditional local techniques of hand-dressing should be limited to conservation and alteration work to historic bridges and to new structures associated with historic structures or environments.

3.9 Load-bearing brick arches and reinforced brick arches should express their form simply. Unnecessary ornamental piers, panels, mouldings and brick patterning should be avoided. Changes in plane of the brickwork, as at string-courses and piers, have the purpose of facilitating and masking changes in the bedding plane of the brickwork.

3.10 Masonry abutments on true arches resist outward thrust by their mass, which can be legitimately expressed by extending above the deck. Large thrust blocks beyond the abutment proper can also be used, and again should be expressed. Penetration through the abutments should be expressed as small openings, to avoid diminishing the apparent mass.

3.11 Stone blocks, being three-dimensional, can be readily cut to form three-dimensional planar bridge geometries. If ashlar stone is to be used, this should be expressed and exploited. Random and coursed rubble stonework lends itself to simpler geometries in section, but can curve in plan with ease, which can be useful in wing walls.

3.12 Where true stone arches are used for civic reasons, decoration is sometimes called for. Only a consultant architect of the highest quality should be used to design this, and one sensitive to that approach to design. A suitable place for elaboration might be a date or coat of arms on the keystone or abutment. Otherwise decoration should be limited to

3.14a (left) PILGRIM'S WAY BRIDGE, Guildford. This was designed to make the total arch the dominant feature, and not to appear as a mousehole.

3.14c (below) PARABOLIC ARCH, Bodegas Guell, Garraf, Spain: structurally the most efficient form.

3.14b (below) LOSTWITHIEL BRIDGE, Cornwall. The pointed arch is structurally more efficient at these proportions.

3.15a (above) PONTE DELLE COLONE, Venice, Italy: chain arch bridge, with flexible structure for poor ground.

non-structural parts, such as balustrades, lampposts or sculpture on top of massive abutments expressing that mass (see also Chapter 23).

3.13 The structure of masonry bridges can act in four ways, which give different visual characteristics: semicircular arches, chain arches, flat segmented arches and balance thrust arches.

3.14 *Semicircular arches* are the simplest form and use voussoirs, often of large proportions. The spandrel infill acts as a mass to prevent deflection and upward movement. Pointed Gothic arches give a closer approximation to the parabolic shape which would theoretically take the loads most directly downwards. The spandrels should be expressed separately from the arch to visually explain the structure, and the depth of the voussoirs not less than one-tenth of the clear span. In small medieval pointed arch bridges, the piers are about the same width as the clear spans, since the mass helps compact the ground.

3.15 *Chain arches* are intended to be highly flexible and consist of a series of long blocks of stone morticed into

transverse blocks about which they can rotate. The spandrel infill is flexible and thus permits settlement and distortion of the structure. They are useful where foundations are very poor, but only suitable for footbridges. The finishes of the spandrels should permit movement and crack repairing.

3.16a (right) Egton Bridge, North Yorkshire: constructed 1994.

3.15b (below) Thames Footbridge, Bloomers Hole, Buscot, Gloucestershire: proposed chain arch design.

3.16b (above) New Brig, Stirling, Central Region, Scotland. Heavy piers needed to resist the arch thrust should be expressed as on this segmental arch.

3.16c (left) Ponte Santa Trinitá, Florence, Italy. Cartouche masks point of shallow arch.

3.16 *Flat segmental arches* give a low rise to span but generate more outward thrust; they can suffer from problems with excessive load in the haunches from the infill, and from excessive flatness at the crown. The spandrels and/or haunches can be pierced to relieve the load and help flood relief on river bridges, and the expression of this can improve the appearance of the bridge. The outward thrust is traditionally resisted by the weight of the piers and abutments, the thickness of which therefore is often between a quarter and one-fifth of the clear span. Extra weight can be obtained by continuing the pier as a cutwater or pedestrian reserve beyond the face of the parapet, and/or continuing it upwards as an obelisk, sculpture or – traditionally – a gatehouse or chapel. This form of construction makes each arch of a multi-span bridge separately stable, permitting sequential construction and easing subsequent repair.

Three-centred arches and ellipses have the advantage of giving smooth lines to flow into the piers, but give weak crowns, both structurally and visually, since the voussoirs cannot radiate from the centres without restraint cramps or joggled joints. Four-centred arches with a small point at the crown are sometimes considered more structurally stable, as on the Ponte Santa Trinitá in Florence. A rise-to-span ratio of 1:7 can be achieved.

3.17a (left)
PONT DE LA
CONCORDE,
Paris, France.
The light piers
of balanced
thrust arches
should be
expressed
as here.

3.17 *Balanced thrust arches* avoid the need for heavy piers by balancing the thrust of one arch of a multi-span bridge against the next, so that the pier only takes the vertical load. The piers can have a thickness of one-tenth of the clear span. This gives a very different character and should be expressed, as on the Pont de la Concorde, Paris. It also enables the arch to be shallower since the horizontal thrust can be taken more easily. Rise-to-span ratios of 1:10 have been achieved. There are technical difficulties, such as having to build all arches at the same time and dropping the centring simultaneously, and the abutments need to be massive to resist the higher loads caused by flatter arches (see Paragraph 3.10 above). The voussoirs should preferably extend across the entire face of the bridge with no expressed spandrels, since this reflects structural necessity and gives strong character.

3.18 All masonry structures compensate for changes in temperature by changing geometry and stresses in the material and by cracking. Movement joints and bearings are therefore unnecessary and visually undesirable in both single-span and multi-span bridges.

PICTURE CREDITS
3.3a d Jonathan Ellis Miller/Mott MacDonald. **3.5a d** IK Brunel; ph JW. **3.7a d** Robert Taylor; ph JW. **3.8a** ph JW. **3.10a** ph JW. **3.11a d** Thomas Telford; ph JW. **3.11b d** Thomas Telford; ph JW. **3.14a d** Edwin Lutyens; ph Bill Smyth. **3.14b** ph JW. **3.14c d** Antonio Gaudí and Francesco Beranguer; ph JW. **3.15a** ph Rowland J Mainstone. **3.15b d** ph Whitby and Bird. **3.16a d** North Yorkshire County Council. **3.16b** ph JW. **3.16c d** Bartolomeo Ammanati; ph JW. **3.17a d** Jean-Rodolphe Perronet; ph JW.

Chapter 4
Concrete and steel arches

4.1 Trussed arches and arch-shaped trusses are covered in Chapter 7, so the present chapter deals primarily with arches below the road deck. These tend to be economical when spanning from 50m to 200m, with suitable topography, unless they are very shallow.

4.2 *The structure consists basically of the arch, the deck and usually some supports from the arch to the deck – in that order of importance. These elements should be expressed in both form and detail, and with due regard for their hierarchy.*

4.3 The soffit of the arch should be expressed in its entirety, not masked by the deck at the crown of the arch.

4.4 Any supports from the arch to the deck should be subservient to both, generally by being more slender and by being recessed from the face of the arch, and possibly of different cross-section, e.g. circular or elliptical, although slender leaf piers are generally the most appropriate for concrete. They are best vertical. If a steel arch is used, efforts should be made to preserve the cleanness of the design by the utmost simplification of the spandrel bracing.

4.2a (top) A27 SHOREHAM BRIDGE, West Sussex: arch, deck and supports expressed hierarchically.

4.4a (above) PONT SULLY, Paris: distinction between arch and supports in spandrels clearly expressed.

4.4b (above) PONT DE BOUTILON, River Allier, France. Occasionally deck supports can be non-vertical but then should be detailed as a truss.

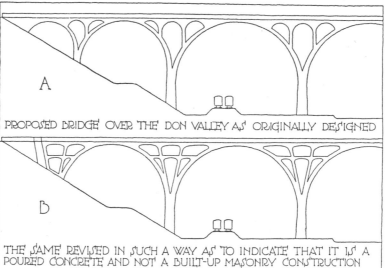

PROPOSED BRIDGE OVER THE DON VALLEY AS ORIGINALLY DESIGNED

THE SAME REVISED IN SUCH A WAY AS TO INDICATE THAT IT IS A POURED CONCRETE AND NOT A BUILT-UP MASONRY CONSTRUCTION

4.4c (right) DON VALLEY VIADUCT. An 'organic' arrangement of supports is also possible.

4.5a (left) A27 BRIGHTON BYPASS, West Sussex: deck as beam plus cantilever (the covers to the bearing pits are obtrusive).

4.6a (left) SMALL CONCRETE BRIDGE DESIGN. The parapet is too heavy and solid for the small arch.

4.7a (below) RUSSIEN ROAD BRIDGE, Switzerland. The face of the arch, deck and supports are best in different planes.

4.7b (below) M25, SEVENOAKS, Kent. Small bridges can have a planar surface.

4.5 Expressing the deck in elevation as beam plus cantilever can make the deck appear more slender and help the visual junction with the arch. The shadow line created by the cantilever should not normally cut across the supporting arch.

4.6 Unless the bridge is very large, a solid parapet should be avoided, since it puts too much emphasis on the deck.

4.7 With open spandrel arches, unless the breadth of the bridge is small, the face of the arch, deck and supports should be in slightly different planes.

4.8 Concrete arches can be either a curved slab or a series of ribs, but steel (or iron) bridges are almost invariably a series of ribs. Ribs will tend to be stouter than a curved plane, and the differences should be considered at the outset.

4.9 The curvature of the arch is generally smooth rather than faceted, though there is a school of thought that says the point loads from the deck supports should make the arch be a series of facets to truly express the loads. This is valid, but it is

also possible to argue that the dead load and also the loads during construction are more evenly distributed and more critical, and therefore the curve is equally valid. Either approach is acceptable, as long as the end result is beautiful. It is particularly difficult to make faceted steel arches appear elegant.

4.10 The support at the springing point of the arch should be seen to transmit the load down to the springing point directly, not just on or just off the arch.

4.8b (left) IRONBRIDGE, Shropshire. Iron and steel arches are always a series of ribs.

4.8c (below) PONT DE NEUILLY, France. Painting the beam edges makes the arch seem more prominent to overcome the widened cantilever.

4.8a (above) TAF FECHAN BRIDGE, Merthyr Tydfil: concrete arch as a series of ribs.

4.9a (below) MESOCCO BRIDGES, Switzerland: elegant, subtly faceted arches.

4.9b (below, right) CLYDEBANK BRIDGE, Duntocher Barn, Scotland: hideous faceted arch with unnecessary crossheads.

4.11 Skew arches and/or horizontally curved decks on arches are best avoided when a curved plane is used and when there are heavy ribs, since it gives unnecessary over-complexity and awkward details. It confuses the clarity of the form.

4.12 Making the abutments square to the bridge may slightly increase the length of the span, which then changes the proportions to a flatter arch. When the bridge is broad relative to its span, therefore, there is less scope for straightening the abutments and removing the skew, especially when the arch is already relatively shallow.

4.13 If there needs to be a skew span, fine ribs, especially in steel, or a thin simple curved plane are best.

Fast-moving viewers passing under an arch do not generally perceive the skew until they are very close.

4.14 With very flat arch bridges on relatively flat ground, it is often better to have a solid abutment beyond the springing point, rather than further open spans. Visually, this gives more of a mass against which the arch appears to thrust. This is the traditional approach for river bridges but is just as valid for road overbridges.

4.15 Slenderness of the arch ring is usually the ideal to be sought. An upstand, inset from the arch ring of concrete curved slab bridges, can stiffen the arch ring and keep it slender. On very shallow concrete arches this upstand

4.11a (left) Spital Bridge, Engstligen, Switzerland. Skewed and twisted spans need extreme skill in designing.

4.14a (below) River Irfon Bridge, Builth Wells, Wales. Shallow steel arch looks correct thrusting against massive abutment.

4.14b (above) Valtschielbach Bridge, Switzerland. Flat arches visually benefit from thrusting against a solid abutment.

4.17a (right) Salginatobel Bridge, Switzerland. For a centre-pinned arch, the thickest zone should be at quarter points of span.

4.15a (above) Zuoz Bridge, Switzerland: possibly the ideal example of a shallow arch with a solid web.

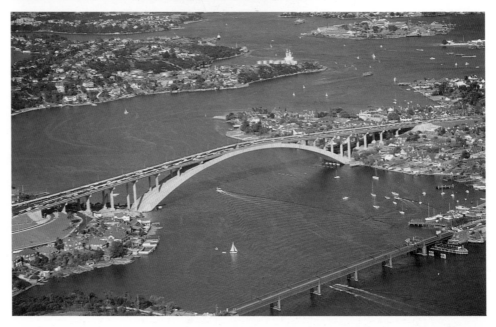

4.17b (right) Gladesville Bridge, Sydney, Australia. For a fixed arch the crown should be the slenderest point.

can form a web to connect to the deck, and can be solid or pierced. Any piercing should reflect the structural action of the web.

4.16 The ratio of arch span to rise should generally be between 2:1 and 10:1. From 4:1 to 10:1 there may be a requirement for a pinned joint or hinge at the springing point and/or sometimes at the crown.

4.17 For an arch pinned at the crown, the two half-arch members should logically be thickest at their centres in both steel and concrete, e.g. the Salginatobel Bridge. For an arch pinned at the bearings, especially a trussed arch, the greatest depth should be at the crown, giving a sickle shape. Unless the arch is parabolic, the bending is at the maximum at the crown, e.g. the Garabit Viaduct (Fig. 7.16b). For a fixed arch, especially in concrete, the crown should be the most slender point.

4.18 A chord drawn between the arch springing points should be parallel to the deck.

4.19 The crown of the arch, and thus the setting-out point for the side span supports, should be vertically above the centre of a chord drawn between the springing points.

4.20 On concrete arches it is best to avoid a gap between the crown of the arch and the deck beam. They are better fused together so that at the crown the centreline of the arch on elevation is tangential to the soffit line of the deck beam. This, therefore, requires the depth of the deck beam to be greater than half the depth of the arch at the crown. For deck-stiffened arches where the arch is very slender, it may be preferable for the top edge of the arch ring to be tangential to the deck beam soffit. But this causes difficult narrow gaps which are unbuildable.

4.21 With steel arches, and concrete arches where there is a gap between the crown of the arch and the deck, there should be an odd number of deck spans over the arch, to avoid having a support at the crown.

4.22 A crossfall or superelevation on the deck should be avoided, since this will increase the depth of the deck and change the overall proportions. A complex but elegant solution is to have the barrel of the arch slightly conical to follow the superelevation in section.

4.23 On high arches, especially when used in a series, it is best to have tall, vertically proportioned openings between deck supports near the springing point to emphasize the height. The piers can also taper in both directions to give a smaller cross-section at the top to emphasize the height.

4.24 If circular or square deck supports are used, their centres across the deck breadth should be less than the centres along the deck. Columns should preferably be in pairs or single, and never more than three across the deck breadth. Deck edge cantilevers and leaf piers should be used to avoid tunnel-like forms on broad bridges (see also Chapter 11).

4.17c (left) Lockyer Creek Bridge, Australia: parabolic arches with slender crowns.

4.21a (right) Arc de Trellins, France. Where the arch does not touch the deck there should be no central support.

4.21b (left) Taf Fechan Bridge, Merthyr Tydfil: dramatic, well-detailed arch.

4.26a (below) OLD ST BERNARD PASS ROAD BRIDGE, Switzerland. Arch-shaped spandrel ribs forming part of a retaining wall can be successful.

4.25a (right) LANGWIESER BRIDGE, Chur, Switzerland: heavy piers at springing now unnecessary.

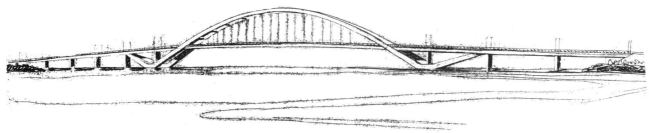

4.28a (above) POOLE HARBOUR CROSSING, Dorset: a suggested proposal. The tied anchorage for the backspan on large tied arches can be difficult to resolve.

4.27a (above, centre) PRINS HENDRIKKADE FOOTBRIDGE, Amsterdam. The deck acts as a tie on this elegant bridge.

4.25 Heavy piers at the springing points should not be structurally necessary if wind loads are taken by a continuous deck, and the visual lightness and transparency of the bridge are enhanced if such heavy piers are omitted. This is true of both single large arches and series of shallow arches, as on a river bridge. If the deck is very long, piers to resist wind loads may be necessary.

4.26 For arch spans between 20m and 40m, vertical walls of an arch shape can be a simple solution, with the deck spanning between the arch-shaped walls, with an edge cantilever. This can work well with bridges or viaducts on a horizontal curvature, where the walls can follow a sinuous line. This form can be used for tall viaducts with stilted arches, but in such cases the outer face is best battered and the piers tapered to a more slender width at the springing point.

4.27 Ties can permit a relatively flat arch where support conditions are inadequate for a true arch. The ties can be concealed underground for road overbridges or for strengthening of historic bridges, but this is generally considered to be dishonest in its expression of structure. The deck can act as the tie at either the springing point or at any point above this. In cross-section there can be two arches, one either side of the deck, either parallel or canted inwards to touch at the crown (Fig. 12.2a). Alternatively, there can be a single arch in the central reservation with cantilevered decks, or a single leaning arch to one side of the deck, balanced by the cantilevered deck (see Chapter 7, Paragraph 7.33).

4.28 With a tied arch, where the deck ties at some distance above the springing point, a cantilevered half-arch shape can be used to support the deck beyond the arch.

4.29a (right) PONT DU MOULIN, France. Diagonal hangers permit a lighter deck.

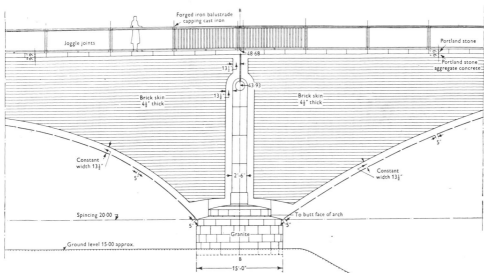

4.30a (left) MAIDSTONE BYPASS BRIDGE, Kent. The real structure should still be expressed in clad arches.

This can look elegant but needs a visually massive pier to terminate and tie down the half arch before any series of approach spans commences. The depth of the deck acting as the tie to the arch should continue as the tie to the cantilevered half arch. It should visually be of a different depth or construction to the approach span deck. Straight struts can be used instead of the curved half-arch cantilever, but whilst structurally logical, there tends to be a visual conflict of form with the main arch.

4.29 Hangers on tied arches are usually vertical in elevation, but inclined hangers triangulating the arch to give a truss action can make the deck more slender.

4.30 When arches are clad, the inherent nature of that particular form of arched bridge should still be expressed, in particular any pin joints and the material of the structure, i.e. concrete or steel (see Chapter 5 for faced arches). Concrete or steel arches should not pretend to be masonry arches.

PICTURE CREDITS
4.2a ph JW. **4.4a** ph JW. **4.4b d** Eugène Freyssinet; ph Jean Muller. **4.4c d** Claude Bragdon. **4.5a** ph JW. **4.6a d** Oscar Faber. **4.7a** ph JW. **4.7b** ph Philip Lane. **4.8a d** Rendel Palmer and Tritton; ph JW. **4.8b d** Thomas Pritchard/Abraham Darby; ph Andrew Cunnisson. **4.8c d** Alain Spielmann; ph JW. **4.9a d** Christian Menn; ph JW. **4.9b d** Owen Williams. **4.11a d** Robert Maillart; ph David Billington. **4.14b d** Robert Maillart; ph David Billington. **4.15a d** Robert Maillart; ph David Billington. **4.17a d** Robert Maillart; ph JW. **4.17b d**/ph Maunsell. **4.21a d**/ph Jean Muller. **4.21b d** Rendel Palmer and Tritton; ph JW. **4.26a** ph JW. **4.27a** ph JW. **4.28a d** Rust Consulting. **4.29a d** Jean Muller. **4.30a d** Charles Holden.

Chapter 5
Faced arches and false arches

5.1 Where a solid arch is constructed in concrete or steel and the vertical faces are finished with stone or brick, these facings should usually express their function.

5.2 The facings may have a number of functions:

- to (partially) support the deck
- to mask structure or services
- to restrict access to the structure
- to protect and simplify access to the structure
- to be more environmentally suitable for the setting.

The latter is possibly the most frequent current reason.

5.3 *In general the facing should not pretend to be the structure, i.e. it should not imitate the voussoirs of a masonry arch.* This does not mean to say that the facing should be expressed as panels stuck onto the face of the bridge. The rectangular stone slabs facing the King George V Bridge in Glasgow detract from the curved geometry of the structure: rectangular cladding is more appropriate to the rectangular geometry of buildings.

5.4 Plain panels of brickwork or random stonework divided by vertical movement joints also detract from the arched form. To the untrained eye the masonry facing *is* the structure, and there is no visual advantage in emphasizing that it is false. It may be the erudite answer, but to many observers it defeats its principal purpose of looking beautiful.

5.3a (above, left) KING GEORGE V BRIDGE, Glasgow. Rectangular slabs emphasize the falseness of the cladding, detracting from the appearance.

5.3b (above, right) WATERLOO BRIDGE, London. Close up, the rectangular slabs mar the appearance, but from a distance they disappear. Structurally this is a variable depth beam.

5.4a (left) TAWE BRIDGE, Pontardawe, Glamorgan. The movement joints, toy pilasters and concrete coping spoil this bridge.

5.5a (right) RUNNYMEDE BRIDGE, River Thames: completed in 1962 to a design by Lutyens, and now carrying the M25. Possibly the finest of Lutyens' bridges.

5.5b (right) MOLE BRIDGE, East Molesey, Surrey: arch, parapet and non-loadbearing spandrels carefully expressed in their details.

5.5c (below) HAMPTON COURT BRIDGE, River Thames: grand civic bridge with structural elements clearly expressed.

5.5d (left) COTT ROAD BRIDGE, Lostwithiel, Cornwall: appropriate rustic design.

5.6a (below) AVON BRIDGE, M40, Warwick. A lack of much detailing gives 'wallpaper' effect.

5.5 It is generally best to express a concrete structural arch by exposing it, then treating the masonry as a wall above it which also expresses the line of the road deck. This also thus defines the parapet as a separate element. The proportions of parapet, spandrel, arch etc. are very important on such bridges.

5.6 When the deck line is not expressed, the scale looks odd due to paucity of detail. Also the coursing of the stone or brick can then follow neither the arch, the deck nor the parapet, so invariably it tends to be horizontal – which can look like wallpaper when not broken up by modelling.

5.7 As with true masonry arches and on retaining walls (Chapter 3 and Chapter 29), the expression of the deck or road line even as a string-course is a useful feature to permit the change of coursing, e.g. from horizontal on the spandrels to following the parapet above.

5.8 The most usual coursing for the spandrels is horizontal, and this can benefit from texture and pattern and particularly from emphasizing the horizontal, which can contrast well with the curves of the arch form. The horizontal banding or emphasis works best with tighter radii rather than very shallow arches.

5.9 A more refined treatment for brickwork, and one which also simplifies the junction between structural arch ring and brickwork, is for the coursing to radiate and step from the ring, emphasizing the arch shape yet not pretending to be structural (Fig. 5.5b). Similarly, voussoir-shaped slabs can be exaggerated and decorative as in Baroque and Islamic architecture, emphasizing that they are a façade. Expressing the fixings of stone slab cladding, e.g. with exposed bolt heads, can be appropriate and attractive.

5.10 When arched bridges are faced, it is very important to mask movement joints, of which there should

5.8a (below) Avenue de Chartres, Chichester, West Sussex.

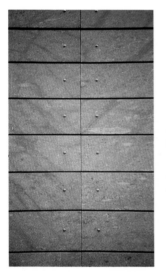 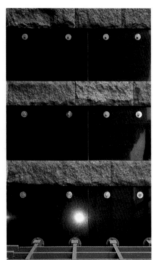

5.9a (above, right) Queen Street, City of London: detail of boldly expressed stonework.

5.9b (above) Stadelhofen, Zürich, Switzerland: detail of exposed bolt heads in stonework cladding.

5.9c (right) Ferdinandsbrücke, Vienna, Austria. Cladding is well expressed by exaggerated arch at foot of decorative clad pier and exposed bolts, though style is no longer appropriate.

5.10a (far left) KING GEORGE V BRIDGE, Glasgow: good abutment detail.

5.10b (left) VAUXHALL CROSS, London: good detailing on river wall.

5.11a (below) COUNTY BRIDGE, Bedford: blatantly false arch to beam bridge.

5.10c (right) COUNTY BRIDGE, Bedford: poor detailing.

be a minimum. At the crown, a keystone or plaque can be appropriate (see Chapter 3, Paragraph 3.12), projecting forward to permit a movement joint behind or in the return corner. At piers or abutments it is best to have the spandrel panel pass behind the projected face of a pilaster or more massive abutment, with the movement joint in the return corner. It is important to keep this joint as small as possible and to have it follow the profile of any mouldings, preferably sealed with a colour-matched mastic joint where movements are not too great. King George V Bridge in Glasgow and the Vauxhall Cross river wall have a successful detail, but the County Bridge, Bedford, draws attention to its falseness and looks about to fall down. Horizontal movement joints should be masked in deep mouldings or other changes of plane.

5.11 The soffit of the facing should always follow the curvature of the structural soffit. The facing should be, and appear to be, attached to the bridge's structure, not hung from the deck like a curtain or projected on brackets from the face of the first structural arch or beam. In other words, it should be an infill between the arched structure and the deck, possibly continuing as a parapet, and not a false façade placed in front of the actual bridge. This is particularly important where people walk under a bridge, and on river and inland waterway bridges (Chapter 14) since the falseness is then very obvious to the slowly moving observer.

5.12 The edge of the structural arch is best expressed on the face but is often improved by using a better finish, like white concrete, a surface treatment such as bush hammering, or a retarder and wash to expose the aggregate. Directional texturing – radial, concentric, vertical or horizontal – should be avoided. It is often more elegant visually to have the expressed arch thinner and attenuated at the crown, to reflect the structural loading. The junction between exposed structure and cladding is very important, especially at abutments.

5.13 There is often a problem of weathering on the concrete arch ring, which detracts from the superior weathering characteristics of brick or stone spandrels. This is made worse by poor detailing, which would allow leakage to be encouraged at vertical movement joints and at balustrade fixing points. Cladding to the arch ring itself is therefore sometimes necessary. This is also the case where the form of the structural arch does not permit exposure, as with corrugated steel culverts, steel structures or 'hole in wall' structures.

5.14 Where the structural arch ring is clad, it is always best to express the arch shape, but rarely best to pretend that the cladding *is* the structure. The shape is usually best expressed radially but should either be exaggerated by modelling or expressed as a thin non-structural trim. Both options avoid confusion with the true structure. This is

particularly applicable where the arch shape or span could not be a true masonry arch for structural reasons.

5.15 *Sometimes, though rarely, it is desirable to pretend that an arched structure is a load-bearing masonry structure when it is not. The use of a true masonry structure should be considered in all such cases, before the decision to proceed with a false structure is made. When in such situations it has been decided that it is necessary to lie, it is very important to lie convincingly, and this is all down to details. Having in situ concrete copings on stone-clad parapets shows they are only a cladding; movement joints in arches destroy the illusion of a structural masonry arch. If it is well detailed, the fact that the appearance does not show it to be a steel or concrete arch is irrelevant.*

In many ways, attention to detail when bridges or abutments are clad to imitate load-bearing masonry is even more important than normal. To lose movement joints by using false joints, the real and false joints must be the same width, depth and colour. Voussoirs must appear structurally logical, be large enough to appear able to span (unlike on the King George V Bridge, Glasgow, Fig. 5.3a) and have visibly believable abutments. Cladding stones must be three-dimensional at all arrises, both on abutments and particularly for voussoirs, where they should project well

5.12a (right) A40 Bridge, Crockers Ash, Hereford & Worcester: elegant arch for viewing at speed.

5.14a (above) Vauxhall Cross, London: River Effra culvert. False voussoirs deliberately exaggerated.

5.14b (above) Avenue de Chartres, Chichester, West Sussex: bridge to car park. Brickwork deliberately not pretending to be an arch.

5.15a (below) Maerdy Bridge, Snowdonia, Gwynedd: precast voussoirs, but the deception is almost perfect.

5.15b (below) Pont de la Tournelle, Paris: false but well-detailed 'masonry arch'.

5.16a (above) Pont Alexandre III, Paris, France: embellishment inappropriate today.

under the soffit. If precast artificial stone is to be used (it is not recommended), especially in conjunction with natural stone, the surface texture should be taken from natural stones with rubber moulds, and the colour adjusted and toned with additives and surface treatments. Techniques developed for theme parks and film sets can be exploited. If an arch shape is used, the proportions must be believable, i.e. not shallower than a 1:10 height-to-span ratio. The advice in Chapter 3 must be followed to produce a believable structure.

Honest engineers and architects usually find such false structures anathemas, but the public can find them prettier than everyday honest structures, so their use may be justified. Whilst not recommending this approach, it is thus appropriate to give the advice in this paragraph.

5.16 Cast-iron embellishments to arched bridges are no longer appropriate, nor currently have any useful function. Lightweight cladding materials such as GRP are inappropriate for faced-arch bridges due to their short life, excessive movement requiring large joints, poor weathering, sheen, colour and hollowness.

PICTURE CREDITS
5.3a ph JW. **5.3b d** Sir Giles Gilbert Scott; ph JW. **5.4a** ph JW. **5.5a d** Edwin Lutyens; ph JW. **5.5b d** Edwin Lutyens; ph JW. **5.5c d** Edwin Lutyens; ph JW. **5.5d** ph JW. **5.6a** ph JW. **5.8a d** Birds Portchmouth Russum; ph JW. **5.9a d** Terry Farrell; ph JW. **5.9b d** Santiago Calatrava; ph JW. **5.9c d** Otto Wagner. **5.10a** ph JW. **5.10b d** Terry Farrell; ph JW. **5.10c** ph JW. **5.11a** ph JW. **5.12a** ph JW. **5.14a d** Terry Farrell; ph JW. **5.14b d** Birds Portchmouth Russum; ph JW. **5.15a** ph JW. **5.15b d** Lucien Deval; ph JW. **5.16a** ph JW.

Chapter 6
Beam and slab bridges

6.1 Bridge engineers must appreciate that the aesthetic considerations most easily demonstrated on large structures are equally important in more modest forms. Members of the public, be they long-distance travellers, commuters or local residents, will regularly view such bridges and they deserve structures which look as good as can sensibly be afforded.

6.2 The choice and type of bridges and viaducts are influenced by alignment, topography, urban or rural setting, materials and economics. Construction is usually in steel or concrete. Many crossings of small rivers, railways or existing roads will lead towards a choice between precast concrete and steel beams. In other situations, in situ construction gives the designer more flexibility in choice of section-shape and provision for vertical and horizontal curvature.

6.3 *For continuous viaduct construction, an aesthetically pleasing result is best achieved by the superstructure reflecting*

6.1a (left) M40, WARWICK. Strong emphasis on the fascia beam running from end to end and the recessive nature of the piers make for a light and open appearance. The properties of the openings have less importance with open ends and underplayed piers.

6.2b (below) STEEL THROUGH DECK, New York Road, Leeds.

6.2a (above, centre) M BEAM BRIDGE: U beam used at the edge to give a vertical plain finish over the beam depth.

6.3a (above) ST CLOUD BRIDGE, Paris: neat and wide box reflecting flowing alignment of roadway.

6.3b (right) MOTORWAY VIADUCT, Rome: multitude of girders on wide supports, giving a cluttered and heavy appearance.

6.3c (right)
River Yare
Viaduct,
Norwich Bypass.
Girder support
within depth of
superstructure
avoids use of
wide supports,
but the soffit is
still relatively
cluttered.

6.4a (below) River Camel
Viaduct, Wadebridge, Cornwall:
simple constant-depth girder
viaduct with clean, neat lines.

6.4c (bottom) A49 Pont La Roire:
a constant depth but visually
interesting soffit.

6.4b (below) A9 Dornoch Firth
Bridge, Scotland: constant-depth
box on simple supports, a low-key
solution suiting a shallow estuarial
crossing. However, the use of
incremental launching has
produced a deep deck in relation
to the span and height above
the water.

the flowing alignment of the roadway. The use of a few wide
hollow or solid beams and box girders is preferred to a
multitude of precast beams or I-section steel girders which
require wide supports. Box-girder construction, especially in
concrete, enables the junction of slip roads and intersections
to be handled sensitively; this is not possible with individual
precast concrete or steel I-section girders.

6.4 The simplest construction type is the constant-depth
beam or girder, and with steel or prestressed concrete
large spans are possible. Continuity enables shallower depths
to be achieved and avoids the numerous expansion joints
which are a source of water penetration and potential staining
and maintenance problems.

ALIGNMENT

6.5 The road alignment over a bridge can affect its
appearance fundamentally. On smaller bridges a
straight, horizontal alignment, avoiding curvature and varying
superelevation, is most easily accommodated, and the soffit
resulting from it when viewed in elevation from below will be
seen as a constant dark strip, and will therefore go relatively
unnoticed. A severe superelevation will, however, expose
much more soffit to a viewer on the raised side. Horizontal
curvature can add drama and interest to a structure, but when
the alignment is curved, particularly on smaller bridges, the
soffit may appear twisted and unsatisfactory. This effect will
be further exacerbated by vertical curvature adding more

visible soffit. Most particularly, varying superelevation will twist a constant-depth bridge and should be avoided where possible.

6.6 *Matters of alignment are generally determined by the highway engineer, so it is important that the bridge designer works closely with the highway engineer at this early stage to ensure that the most appropriate solutions are found* (see Chapter 2).

6.7 Curvature is not readily accommodated by simple beams. Those in prestressed concrete will always be straight in plan and have nominal hog in elevation. Steel beams, however, can be fabricated with reasonable vertical curvature as well as horizontal curvature. Welded joints give clean and simple lines, but bolted splices can be entirely acceptable if the bolts are well organized. If straight beams are used on a horizontally curved bridge, the curved edge cantilever will cast an unsatisfactory 'scalloped' shadow line on the beam. With a curved vertical alignment, generally straight beams must not be allowed to give an appearance of breaking their backs over a support. The alignment of the beam soffit and, most particularly, the fascia beam must be curved smoothly to reflect the curvature of the road.

6.8 Severe longitudinal falls in a structure can make the bridge visually disturbing. Careful asymmetric design can lead to an appealing structure utilizing the change of shape and size of openings to advantage.

SPANS

6.9 The numbers of spans will often be dictated by the location, but the designer usually has freedom to choose between open or closed end spans. An odd number of spans is usually preferable to an even number (unless there is a central reservation pier on a dual carriageway), with the end span being up to 0.8 times the internal span. Open end spans on

bankseat abutments are generally preferable in rural settings to give an open aspect to the bridge in elevation and to seek to make the deck flow into the top of the embankment. The bankseat should be unobtrusive and not break the line of the deck into the embankment.

6.10 In an urban streetscape, the mass of the structure will normally be kept as small as possible. The superstructure should be slender, with shallow faces – vertical or inclined – to beams, girders, fascia beams and parapets. A vertical abutment can be used with brickwork or other cladding to integrate the structure into its environment. Nevertheless, with many new roads seeking to open up areas for development along a landscaped corridor, the open end span may still be the more appropriate solution.

6.11 In a rural setting the span and depth of construction are governed by the topography and nature of the countryside. In mountainous and steeply sided valleys, relatively small spans with tall columns will enhance the feeling of height (Fig. 11.6f). In wider valleys longer spans with rectangular proportions will give a more pleasing appearance. For long, low viaducts, a shallow superstructure with relatively short spans and flat rectangular proportions of openings will again give a more pleasing appearance. Vertical or horizontal rectangles for openings are preferable to square openings.

6.12 Two-span structures, traditionally considered to suffer from problems of unresolved duality when crossing rivers, are now becoming more readily acceptable for road overbridges. As there is no central span to act as a focus for the observer, the central pier should have visual interest or the deck should be caused to flow easily over it so that this central support becomes less obtrusive. With large vertical curvature the central pier can look like a prop supporting a drooping deck.

6.7a (above, left) STRAIGHT BEAM WITH CURVED PARAPET: an unsatisfactory combination.

6.7b (above) M4, BOSTON MANOR: sagging shadows on straight girders from curved deck.

6.12a (left) M40, WARWICK: two-span accommodation bridge.

6.14a (left) Derma Corniche, Libya: variable curve soffit.

6.18a (below) A64 York Bypass. The curved soffits reduce the oppressiveness of a bridge which is very low over the river banks.

6.16a (above) Mound Bridge, Scotland: splayed leg portal.

SUPERSTRUCTURE

6.13 *The slenderness of the beam remains the most important criterion.* The slenderness ratio, 1/d (span divided by depth), will generally be between 20 and 30 for spans exceeding 10m. The numbers of beams and therefore their spacing will affect the achievable ratio, but they should not be so closely spaced that reasonable access for inspection and maintenance is prevented.

6.14 On larger bridges the apparent depth can be reduced by using a narrow main beam or girder, and large cantilevers with shallow parapet height. A darker tone of colour on the beam can accentuate this effect, and the apparent depth and feeling of lightness can be further improved by a variable curved soffit which disguises the depth of superstructure.

6.15 Structural continuity is important for maintenance reasons. It prevents water and salt penetration through leaking joints, thereby reducing the potential for staining. It also has benefits in aesthetic terms by giving visual continuity to the deck over-supports and by requiring only a single bearing at pier supports.

6.16 A portal frame has apparent strength and structural continuity. It can be formed in situ, allowing expression in shape and curvature, or by casting in precast beams to become integral with the walls. Portal legs can be hidden (Fig. 6.31a). Splay-legged portals may also be attractive, though the legs must not infringe the required headroom clearance envelope at road underbridges.

6.17 The light below very wide dual carriageway viaducts should be improved by carrying the carriageways on independent superstructures with an opening along the central reserve to allow the light through.

6.18 The edge detailing of the deck beams, the parapet cantilever and the fascia beam are important factors in giving the bridge a satisfactory appearance. The outer faces of concrete beams and slabs should have a plain vertical or sloping finish, and their corners can be rounded to make the beam depth appear indefinite. Steel beams should not be cluttered by stiffeners, and fabrication should be controlled to minimize web distortion.

6.19a (left) M40 Hatton Railway
Bridge: concrete parapet over
railway span only.

6.20a (below) Cross-section of
Bridge Deck. The proportions
recommended follow a study by
Cardiff University School of
Engineering.

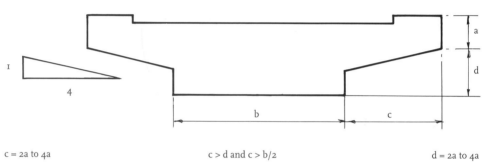

c = 2a to 4a   c > d and c > b/2   d = 2a to 4a

DECK INCLINATION   1 IN 4 OR LESS

6.19 On concrete bridges, edge cantilevers can be from zero to several metres depending upon the form of construction. A slab bridge may have a vertical face and in situ concrete parapet above, so that there is no cantilever. This type of bridge can have a very heavy appearance. It may be considered at railway crossings where heavy concrete parapets are required. In these locations the definition of the deck and parapet can be identified by surface texturing. In most circumstances, the greater the cantilever, the greater the benefit in reducing the visual depth of the deck.

6.20 The cantilever minimizes the visual effect of depth in the superstructure by casting shadow onto the main beam structure and hence emphasizing the light on the fascia beam. The eye of the observer is thereby drawn to the line of the fascia beam, to its continuity over intermediate supports and abutments, and on into the ground line behind. Ideally, the cantilever will be about twice the depth of the beam supporting it, but this may not be achievable with some forms of construction.

6.21 The height of the string-course beam itself can be controlled by the designer. The level of the top of the beam will be determined by crossfall of the verge or footway over the bridge, but the underside of the beam can be varied at the designer's discretion. Drawings and models should be used to get this right. Thus, with larger spans and greater structural depth, the string-course can be extended below the cantilever to mask the supporting structure.

6.22 The quality of finish of the outer face of the fascia beam is critical to the appearance of the finished structure. The top face should be sloped inwards sufficiently to ensure that water runs onto the deck, not down the outer face. There should be sufficient reinforcement in the beam to prevent large cracks appearing due to early thermal shrinkage, and it may need to be placed outside shear links to get it close enough to the corners and exposed faces. To control further this cracking, the fascia beam can also be jointed in alternate bays of the steel or aluminium parapet above. It is not possible to prevent all cracking in these cantilevers and fascia beams, but it is necessary to ensure that all cracks are small. Large ones are most visible after rain, when the plain surface has dried but water remains in the crack. This is most obtrusive and unacceptable.

6.23 Water runoff is further controlled by drip grooves under the fascia beam. They must be deep, wide and continuous. Good control on site will be required to ensure that grout in joints and at other locations does not leave a permanent bridge across the groove.

6.24 The control of water through any bridge is important. It may penetrate joints, service bays, ducts and other features, and will thus be capable of staining concrete faces, causing washout around abutments or forming into stalagtites. Good drainage details must be developed to counteract the tendency for this to happen.

6.25 The fascia beam is usually cast with a vertical face, but this can be sloped a little to catch light more readily. Curved, rounded or aerofoil string-courses or edge details give a softer edge but less clarity of arris, especially in overcast conditions.

VARIABLE-DEPTH BEAMS

6.26 Haunched beams can be very attractive in appropriate locations. They can be formed either by straight haunches local to an intermediate support, or by curvature through the entire length of internal spans and the bridge side of end spans.

6.27 Straight haunches are appropriate where the over-road is straight and horizontal or on a slight incline. It is recommended that they should not exceed approximately one-quarter the span length or be too steeply inclined. Steep haunches giving greatly increased depth at the pier are usually unsatisfactory.

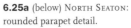
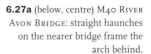

6.27a (below, centre) M40 RIVER AVON BRIDGE: straight haunches on the nearer bridge frame the arch behind.

6.25a (below) NORTH SEATON: rounded parapet detail.

6.27b (below) RIVER MEDWAY BRIDGE M20: straight haunches on visually a two-span bridge – a heavy appearance.

6.27c (bottom) ATHLONE BYPASS BRIDGE, Ireland. A shallow deck, straight haunches extended into piers, and broad, shallow cutwaters combine to give a strong and distinctive effect.

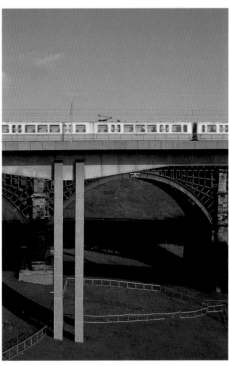

6.27d (above) BYKER VIADUCT, Tyne & Wear Metro. Tall, slender, divided piers, straight haunches and a shallow deck.

6.28a (top) ORWELL BRIDGE, Ipswich. The main span is expressed by the curved soffit.

6.28b (above) M25 ACCOMMODATION BRIDGE.

6.28c (right) ROQUEBILIÈRE VIADUCT, Cahors, France. Curved haunches on main span contrast with straight spans.

6.29b (below, right) GRETA BRIDGE, Keswick: inclined sides to box.

6.28 Curved haunches giving a parabolic shape between intermediate supports are most acceptable when the vertical alignment is curved around a summit, or for the main span of a river crossing between shorter side spans. A slenderness ratio, l/d, of about 50 can be achieved at midspan to give a very slender and elegant structure.

6.29 With the attraction of forces to the haunch at the intermediate support, it is necessary that the pier should be visually strong to support the haunch, or the haunch should visually rest on the surface without a pier. The perceived flow of forces towards the pier requires the

6.29a (above) TORRIDGE BRIDGE, Devon: vertical sides to box.

intermediate support to appear directly under the thrust of the haunch. The outer edge of a haunch should never appear unsupported or it will look like a frilly pelmet.

6.30 Side spans may have a straight or curved soffit. If curved, the end spans should normally have the same or similar parabolic curve on the inner end of the span but should become parallel with the string-course from midspan to the abutment.

6.31 A single-span construction with a curved soffit in a rock cutting can be very effective. The flow of forces from the curved deck into the strong rock face gives simplicity and clarity. Rock cuttings in general often give opportunities for ingenuity and the use of less common forms of construction.

6.32 Skew effects can make curved soffits unacceptable. The curvature combined with the skew exposes more soffit than a straight bridge and this becomes visually disturbing. It

is particularly noticeable with precast concrete or steel beam construction, where the observer also starts to see up between the beams.

INTERMEDIATE SUPPORTS

6.33 *Shaping intermediate supports probably gives designers more freedom of choice than any other aspect. A thin pier supporting a heavy superstructure looks unsatisfactory and inadequate, even though it may be structurally correct. Similarly, a heavy pier supporting a light deck is unsatisfactory.*

6.34 Walls are most easily detailed but the ends may be shaped in longitudinal and transverse elevations and in plan. In end elevation, vertical faces are preferred, but the tapering of a wall in elevation viewed from under the bridge will help to reduce the apparent mass. This is particularly appropriate on wide bridges.

6.29c (left) Costa e Silva Bridge, Brazil: dramatic flat curves over water.

6.29d (left, centre) M1/North Circular Road Junction, London. Unsupported edge gives 'frilly pelmet' appearance.

6.29e (below) Lower Lea Bridge, London: well-defined support, spoiled by inset bearing.

6.31a (left) Greatwood Footbridge, Brighton Bypass: attractive use of curved soffit giving light appearance.

6.35a (below) Viaduc du Maf: tall, dramatic piers, split longitudinally through their full height.

6.35b (right) Byker Viaduct, Newcastle upon Tyne: tall piers with openings near the base only, to reduce obstruction.

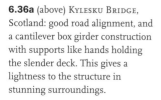

6.36a (above) Kylesku Bridge, Scotland: good road alignment, and a cantilever box girder construction with supports like hands holding the slender deck. This gives a lightness to the structure in stunning surroundings.

6.37a (centre, right) M25 Berry Lane Viaduct: concrete columns blending with trees.

6.37b (right) A54 Petit Rhône Bridge, Arles, France: interesting expression in the pier support.

6.35 The tall pier columns of high viaducts are dominant features which need to be handled sensitively. Their shape and proportions must be harmonious when seen from a distance and must be sympathetic with the superstructure. The width of the pier columns should be the same as the width of the superstructure soffit, and it is preferable that the columns should be tapered. With very tall piers the tapering is best only or mainly in the lower third (see Fig. 11.6f). Twin piers or split piers can help the slender appearance. Access doors into piers and abutments, and bearing galleries need to be carefully detailed.

6.36 Specific locations may require special forms of construction, and this should be visually celebrated (Fig. 2.3a).

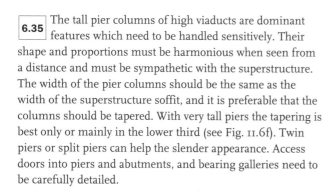

6.37 If possible, the pier support on wide bridges should be broken up to allow light and openness, either by two or three basically rectangular supports or by individual columns. A forest of supports should be avoided, though a number of columns with similar proportions can blend with surrounding trees. By contrast, a strongly defined support can be very expressive. Ellipse or super-ellipse shapes will often be better visually than rectangles with semicircular or other shaped ends. An odd number of columns is preferable, and the space between them should not be equal to the size of the column. Square columns are generally unsatisfactory in appearance, except when they are very tall and tapered to emphasize their height. They do not work well on skewed structures. Columns can be shaped and textured, particularly in an urban landscape, giving scope for more interesting modelling. This can be useful in a pedestrian environment.

6.38 The use of a hammerhead to support precast or prefabricated beams can be difficult. The hammerhead usually looks heavy and visually disruptive, so where possible it should be built into the depth of the beams in the superstructure or tapered so that the end elevation is minimized.

6.39 The same form of intermediate support should normally be used at all locations (Fig. 9.9a).

6.40 On a typical highway scheme there may be several overbridges, which should be designed as a family with consistency of form for the varying geometric requirements. When designing such a family of structures, the effects of skew on the piers should be considered. What appears satisfactory on a square crossing may be quite inappropriate at a high skew.

END SUPPORTS

6.41 End supports will be either bankseat or skeleton abutments in most rural situations, or full-height closed abutments with large wingwalls may be appropriate in some urban settings. The choice will be dependent upon the local environment. In urban or industrial areas it may be appropriate to consider brick or stone cladding to integrate the structure into the locality. Guidance on choice of cladding is given in Chapter 20. Plain concrete finishes should always be

6.38a (below) MOTORWAY VIADUCT, Sydney: integral crosshead in precast beam construction.

6.38b (below) A1 BLAYDON HAUGHS VIADUCT, Newcastle upon Tyne: integral crosshead in steel construction.

6.41a (left) M5 SWAN LANE OVERBRIDGE, Worcester: closed abutments in rural settings. It is preferable that the apparent mass of the abutments is minimized.

6.41b (bottom, left) INCLINED ABUTMENTS: again, heavy in appearance. Horizontal emphasis in the finish is usually preferable.

6.41c (below) OPEN-SIDE SPAN: generally preferable in a rural setting.

6.42a (left) TORRIDGE BRIDGE, Devon. Small abutments add elegance to bridge but access doors in end support are repainted an inappropriate colour and made too prominent.

avoided on larger faces such as wingwalls. Continuity of finish details using relief and/or texture can be used to relate the end and intermediate supports.

6.42 End supports must relate to the overall structure in the flow of lines and give continuity of finishes between the relevant parts. The lines of the fascia beam, for instance, should flow from the deck through the abutment.

6.43 Where bearings are required, masking walls can be omitted at the ends of bearing shelves to clearly define the support of the deck. The need for access to bearings and joints requires space to be created around them: this gives the designer the opportunity to emphasize in elevation the transition between supporting and supported structures, while using the strong continuing lines of the fascia beam to maintain the flow of the deck through to the embankment.

6.44 Wingwalls on full-height closed abutments can be in line with the over-road or the under-road, or be angled part way between the two. Landscaping and planting can be used to mask walls in line with the over-road, whereas walls in line with the under-road will only be visible in end elevation to people approaching the structure. The latter are particularly inconspicuous beside rail tracks. Where the road over is on embankment and the road under in cutting, the wing walls can be split at the natural ground level to render each part and the whole less obtrusive.

PICTURE CREDITS
6.1a d Arup; ph JW. **6.2a** ph Arup. **6.2b** ph JW. **6.3a d**/ph Jean Muller/ Alain Spielmann. **6.3b** ph Arup. **6.3c d** Maunsell; ph Paul Clifford. **6.4a d** Gifford & Partners; ph Neil Lindsay. **6.4b d** Tony Gee & Partners. **6.4c d**/ph Jean Muller. **6.7a d** Scott Wilson Kirkpatrick. **6.7b** ph Andrew Cunnison. **6.12a d**/ph Arup. **6.14a d** Howard Humphries. **6.16a d**/ph Halcrow. **6.18a d**/ph Arup. **6.19a d**/ph Arup. **6.20a d** Cardiff University. **6.25a d**/ph Arup. **6.27a d**/ph Arup. **6.27b d**/ph Scott Wilson Kirkpatrick. **6.27c d**/ph Arup. **6.27d d**/ph Arup. **6.28a d**/ph Halcrow. **6.28b d**/ph Mott MacDonald. **6.28c d** Alain Spielmann; ph JW. **6.29a d**/ph Rust. **6.29b d**/ph Scott Wilson Kirkpatrick. **6.29d d**/ph JW. **6.29e d**/ph Mott MacDonald. **6.31a d** Mouchel; ph JW. **6.35a d** Jean Muller. **6.35b d**/ph Arup. **6.36a d**/ph Arup. **6.37a d** Arup. **6.37b** ph Benoit Pesle. **6.38a** ph Arup. **6.38b d**/ph Bullens. **6.41a d**/ph Howard Humphries. **6.41c** ph JW. **6.42a d** Rust; ph JW.

Chapter 7
Trusses and tied arches

7.1 There are a great many different types of truss, a structural form suitable for many materials but especially timber, steel and sometimes concrete. The basic principle is to make a large structure from smaller members. This may be necessary due to problems of erection, access,

weight, wind loading or limitations on available material. All trusses act three-dimensionally in space and are seen in three dimensions due to their relative transparency, but some are designed as flat planes plus bracing whilst others fully exploit the three dimensions.

7.2 Trusses can also form elements of other structures: decks, pylons (Fig. 26.10b), arches and ties; or act integrally with a deck (Fig. 6.4c). But there are basic aesthetic principles for all shapes, materials and uses of trusses.

7.1a (right) HIDA RIVER BRIDGE, Japan: slender, well-proportioned planar truss.

7.2a (below) PONT DE TANCARVILLE, Le Havre, Brittany, France: trussed deck.

7.2b (below, centre) TRANSPORTER BRIDGE, Middlesbrough, Cleveland: dynamic and elegant trussed pylons (see also Fig. 22.15a).

7.2c (above, right) SAKAI BRIDGE, Nagasaki, Japan: dramatic arched truss.

7.2e (above) OBERBAUM BRIDGE, Berlin. Delicacy of new truss adds modern equivalent of Gothic decoration.

7.2d (above) TOWER BRIDGE, London: somewhat illogical trussed ties.

7.3 *Trusses should be visually as light and transparent as possible.*

7.4 Junctions and nodes should be kept visually simple and gusset plates should be avoided if possible.

7.5 Diagonal bars should be parallel to each other; ties should be parallel or radiating from the same point. This should be consistent throughout all parts of the structure (Fig. 10.4a).

7.6 Diagonals are best at either 60°, which gives equal-sided triangles, or at 45° to give diagonal squares and/or crosses, but not both on one structure. This becomes particularly important when the structure is seen at an oblique angle, when such a co-ordinated unity helps avoid confusion and clutter by making all lines seem parallel.

7.7 The ties connecting top chords of through trusses can look unpleasant and should be minimized. They should be at the same angle or at right angles and to the same nodes as the diagonal members of the trusses. When the deck breadth is more than 1.5 times the height of the through truss, the wind bracing can and should be omitted by making the diagonals of the main truss wide enough to restrain the top chord by transverse bending stiffness.

7.8 Any similarity to temporary structures such as Bailey bridges and falsework should be avoided, since this is perceived as ugly by the public and is inappropriate. This can be done by avoiding twin structural members, especially where prefabricated sections join, by simplifying nodes, by avoiding multiple extremely light members, by avoiding I-section steelwork, by co-ordinating lighting and signing with the structure, and by using arched shapes to be site-specific.

7.4a (left) Musée d'Orsay Footbridge, Paris: perfectly pure and simple trussed bridge.

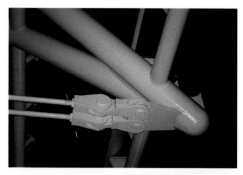

7.4b (left) Railway Station Roof, Chur, Switzerland: elegant truss tie detail (see also 7.20c).

7.5b (left) Railway Bridge, Southwark Street, London. Diagonals should have been of a consistent angle throughout, even if the scale is different.

7.5a (above) Shad Thames, London: simple geometries best.

7.8a (right) Walton Bridge, Surrey: probably the ugliest bridge on the Thames.

7.10a (above)
Guy's Hospital
Footbridge,
London Bridge:
too heavy and
out of scale.

7.10b (above) Cragside,
Northumberland. Timber gives a
more human scale.

7.11a (right)
Francis Scott
Key Bridge,
Baltimore, USA:
a visually
cluttered design.

7.13a (below) Footbridge,
A55 coast road, North Wales. Both
solid panels over railway and
railings over road look good.

7.9 Structural members should intersect on their centrelines generally, but where there is a dramatic difference between thickness of main chords and minor diagonals, the diagonal centrelines can intersect at the face of the major member.

7.10 The amount of detail expressed, especially at junctions, can affect the appearance and scale of the structure. Trusses with flush joints on large members can look very heavy and out of scale, especially with vierendeel trusses. This is particularly so on RHS steel footbridges, where the form is similar to a handrail but much bigger and heavier. More detail to break down the scale is required, e.g. more visually complex junctions, more complexity in member section, or more surface interest such as with timber.

7.11 Main chords and primary diagonals should be of sufficient size to avoid the need for secondary ties, braces or hangers in any plane, since these visually clutter the design especially when seen at oblique angles.

7.12 The cross-sections of members should be consistent, not a mixture of tube, I-section, box section, lattice beam, etc. Consistency gives order and clarity of structure. The exception is where the different structural sections are used to express different structural functions, e.g. on trussed arches (Paragraph 7.18).

7.13 Openings in trusses are best completely open or completely filled, rather than partially filled with a panel or railing.

7.16a (right) New River Gorge Bridge, West Virginia, USA: huge but delicate span.

7.14a (below) British Army Footbridge: timber cable-stayed truss (see Chapter 9).

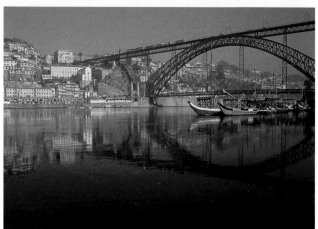

7.16d (above, centre) Douro Bridge, Oporto, Portugal. Two deck levels exploit site.

7.16e (above) Bayonne Bridge, New York: trussed abutments unnecessary and awkward.

7.16b (left, centre) Garabit Viaduct, near Clermont Ferrand, France. Arched trusses were a nineteenth-century phenomenon, now revived.

7.16c (left) Zambezi Gorge Bridge, Africa: dramatic form for a dramatic site.

7.17a (right) HELL GATE BRIDGE, New York: masonry pylon physically connected but structurally inessential to arch.

7.17b (below) SYDNEY HARBOUR BRIDGE, New South Wales: masonry pylon clearly not structural.

7.18b (bottom) G-MEX CENTRE BRIDGE: detail.

7.18a (left) G-MEX CENTRE BRIDGE, Manchester: well-detailed modern arch.

7.14 Trusses of various shapes but which act as beams and true trussed arches are covered in the following paragraphs.

7.15 *Recent research has shown that curved forms and timber are preferable to the public, but many engineers have traditionally disliked trusses. Arched trusses acting mainly as beams and true trussed arches can satisfy both.* Engineering trusses used in recent architecture can provide useful inspiration.

7.16 Arches can be underneath the deck, with trussed towers or rock abutments. They can also be tied arches, with the deck hung below, or combined structures.

7.17 In other types of steel arch, the transverse girders carrying the deck are hung from the arch where it rises above the road and the arch varies in depth dramatically. *If a satisfactory appearance is to be achieved, the arch should be allowed to dominate the rest of the structure.* Early versions of this terminated in pylons projecting above the bridge deck. Whilst visually they terminate the arch well, they are not structurally necessary.

7.18 Tied arches or bowstring trusses can either be tied by the deck, where the arch should visually dominate, or act more as an arched-shaped beam. On such bridges it is particularly important to express the function of the various parts. The arch and tie should be seen to have strength.

Hangars should be expressed as only taking load in tension, i.e. be rods with pinned joints. Where a point load like a hanger transfers load to a plate or other member, strengthening will be required, and it is appropriate to express this. The junction of the arch to tie has heavy loading and this should be expressed.

7.19 There is a family of trusses with arched top booms which may superficially be a similar shape to a tied arch or bowstring truss but act very differently, since all members take approximately similar loads. Care should be taken not to confuse visually the two forms. There is a structural logic in the truss increasing in depth in the centre, but since it is not the top curved boom taking the principal load it is inappropriate to project the curved line of the top boom down beyond the bearing to the ground, either as a member in a

trussed or framed support, or across the face of a concrete or masonry abutment. If a line of structure or change of face material approximates to such a line, visually it is better if that line is a straight tangent to the top boom curve through the apparent bearing point. Santiago Calatrava's proposal for the East London River Crossing (see Fig. 10.1b) illustrates this point, although the concept is a tied arch and cantilever rather than a truss.

7.20 This family of trusses includes those with a trellis of flat bars either on a radiating grid (the Belfast truss) or on a diagonal grid with diagonal members, or with vertical members and stiff joints. The vierendeel truss, a popular form in concrete in the 1930s, now seems appallingly heavy and cumbersome. The form can be light and delicate in steel, however, as can the bicycle-wheel truss.

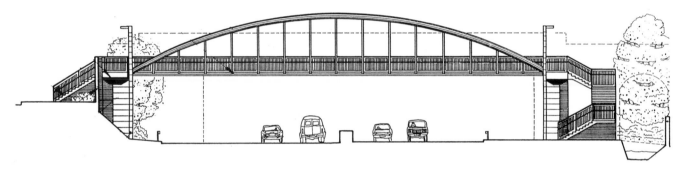

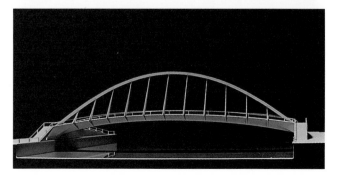

7.19a (top) BOUNDS GREEN FOOTBRIDGE, North Circular Road, North London. Arch stops correctly at abutment.

7.20a (above) TULLA BRIDGE, Glencoe, Scotland: heavy 1930s design.

7.20c (above, centre) RAILWAY STATION ROOF, Chur, Switzerland. Bicycle-wheel truss gives extremely light effect.

7.20b (above) URIBITARTE BRIDGE, Bilbao, Spain: delicate steel design.

7.21a (left) Queen Elizabeth II Bridge, Newcastle upon Tyne: sagging form not recommended.

7.21b (below) Kollstraumen Bridge, Norway: fish belly form, but actually a suspension bridge.

7.22a (below) Cavargna Footbridge, Lombardy, Italy: rustic simplicity similar to a roof truss.

7.22b (left) Embankment Place Footbridge, London: good emphasis on simplicity.

7.21 A similar form but inverted is also possible where there is a good clearance below the deck. This is the fish belly truss, a shape more commonly associated with plate girders, but which has interesting potential. A version where the top boom sags in imitation of a suspension bridge is not recommended.

7.22 Triangular trusses have a simple purity of logic, and can resemble a roof truss for a through truss bridge, or be inverted as on the Embankment Place Footbridge. Some of the finest were by IK Brunel in timber for his Cornish railways. When there is the opportunity to express members in pure tension, i.e. as rods or cables, it should be taken, to produce the most light, transparent and delicate structure.

7.22c (left) Gover Viaduct, Cornwall: tree-like timber trusses.

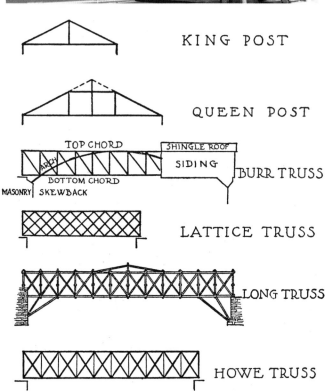

7.24a (left) PADDINGTON FOOTBRIDGE, London: cable-stayed vierendeel. This is relatively light for a vierendeel.

7.24b (below) JEDDAH FOOTBRIDGE, Saudi Arabia: vierendeel with perforated web in Islamic style.

7.24c (bottom) TRADITIONAL AMERICAN TIMBER TRUSS DESIGNS may provide inspiration for new designs.

7.23 Straight trusses are probably the most frequently used and can have advantages over simple beams. They are particularly useful when loads are light, spans are long and wind loads critical. The straight top and bottom booms simplify use. As with all trusses there is the potential (rarely exploited) to remove and replace individual members for maintenance and repair. Their disadvantage is that they tend to be very deep for their span and are inherently not beautiful, especially the through trusses for heavy loads such as railways.

7.24 There are many geometric arrangements for members:
• the simple but heavy vierendeel with moment joints and no diagonals
• a vierendeel with a plain or perforated web panel
• the Howe truss with cross-braced rectangles
• the Pratt truss with diagonally braced rectangles
• the Warren truss with no verticals and zig-zag pattern
• the modified Warren truss with added alternate verticals
• the Fink truss with top boom only, suspended post and diagonal ties
• the diagonally braced truss with no verticals
• the lattice truss
plus many variations and modifications.

7.25 The stiff vierendeel trusses tend to have heavy members but simple lines. The more complex trusses can use smaller and shorter members (useful for timber), and they can also permit the use of rods or cables for tension members, which can add physical and visual lightness to a design, plus more visual interest. This can be of particular importance with footbridges which are seen close up.

7.26 Rectangular steel members with vertical faces tend to have a very heavy appearance and combine with the necessary simple welded joints often to give an overscaled appearance. This is especially so when the truss height on pedestrian through trusses is 1.5m to 2m, and so looks like a handrail for giants. Using square steel sections on their diagonal can give added visual interest due to additional arrises and improved shadow modelling, although junctions need more care taken when detailing is designed.

7.27 Circular section steel members on lightweight structures such as footbridges can tend to look too light and flimsy, since the modelling from shadows makes them appear more slender than they actually are. Selecting a geometric arrangement which requires longer and stouter members, or using larger diameter tubes with thinner walls, can overcome this problem. Welded joints at intersections of members can look very elegant if carefully manufactured and if the geometry is carefully thought out (see Paragraph 7.9). Bolted connections such as in-line splices should not project

beyond the face of the tube. Ear plates for bolting ties of a different diameter, e.g. rods, should be rounded with curves centred on the intersection point or the pin of a pin joint.

7.28 L- and I-section steel and castellated beams should generally be avoided for truss members, since they have connotations of temporary structures. Perforated steel I-sections are generally an architectural affectation originally developed to lighten members and facilitate building services. All of these should only be used with the utmost caution and with the advice of a top-quality architect.

7.29 Timber is an excellent material for trusses visually, particularly for pedestrian bridges. Its natural texture and visual attractiveness, combined with the structural necessity of expressing the joints by bolts, brackets or lapping, give a human scale and appropriate gentle organic imagery particularly suitable to the countryside. Even when large structural timbers are used the scale tends not to be oppressive due to the surface visual interest and the finite limit on the size of both natural and laminated timber. Traditionally in Europe and America such bridges were often clad and roofed to protect the structure and decrease snowloading. This is now rare. The American railway system used predominantly timber trusses, often in piers. Timbers of large section and length

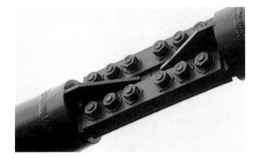

7.27a (right) IN-LINE SPLICE DETAIL: carefully designed to be within tube diameter.

7.29a (above) PONS RUSSIEN, Switzerland: note recent post-tensioned strengthening.

7.29b (above) GASWORKS BRIDGE ROAD, Gateshead, Tyne & Wear: excellent large modern timber truss bridge.

7.29c (above) SCOTTISH FOOTBRIDGE: proprietary elegant design.

7.30a (left) FOOTBRIDGE: delicate and unusual timber fink truss bridge.

7.31a (left) A5 VIADUCT, Val d'Aosta, Italy: concrete truss module. Concrete trusses are rare but can be successful.

7.33b (right) LA DEVESA BRIDGE, Rippoll, Spain: stylish leaning mono-planar tied arch.

7.33a (bottom, right) MEPPEN BRIDGE, Germany: mono-planar truss.

have become increasingly difficult to obtain this century, therefore laminated timber and truss formats with larger numbers of smaller members have become more appropriate.

7.30 Timber truss bridges are best detailed to incorporate timber parapets and handrails. Preservative-treated timber, or that not requiring it such as oak, is preferable to painted finishes, which need more maintenance and mask the wood's natural appearance. Detailing must avoid producing pockets which might trap water. Natural materials weather and mellow inconsistently. They warp and twist as they dry out, and some timber such as oak and certain pines weeps tannin or resin when new. Large section timber also can develop shakes along the fibres. All of this is natural and part of the character of timber, but should be allowed for when detailing. Such changes are not normally of any structural significance, though each case should be judged on its merits.

7.31 Concrete trusses, though once popular, are generally very heavy and ugly. Lightness, the truss's principal visual attraction, cannot normally be exploited in concrete due to the minimum thickness required to protect reinforcement. There is some potential with precast elements, particularly using three-dimensional geometry and GRC for thin shells and fine quality finishes. The smooth, flowing curves which can express concrete's cast nature are best exploited in such trusses.

7.32 All shapes and materials of trusses can be mono-planar, multi-planar or three-dimensional.

7.33 Mono-planar structures have one truss, either below or above the deck. When above, it is generally in the central reservation to give a balanced structure, so is only viable for dual carriageways. The simplicity of the single deck and elegance of its cantilever should be emphasized, and can give a very slender edge to the deck, visual interest underneath and an elegant sculptural form overall. Concentration of all loads in one truss makes this form one of the most suitable for concrete. For smaller structures with a single carriageway or only a footpath it is possible to tilt the truss from the vertical and cantilever the deck from one side so that the loads are balanced. This can be extremely elegant and very dramatic, but having to cope with torsion and the relative complexity of the structural design has discouraged many engineers from using this simple form.

7.34 Multi-planar structures are the most common, e.g. twin or triple through girders. Where they need to be braced against each other, as for wind load, it is best to avoid confusion with true three-dimensional structures. Planar linearity should be emphasized and bracing expressed with a different size, shape, orientation or colour of member.

7.35 Three-dimensional trusses in cross-section are generally triangular, rectangular, pentagonal or circular. They can also be simultaneously curved in elevation, giving for instance a sector of a sphere or a more asymmetric geometric solid. Triangular sections are inherently strong and exploit the particular visual characteristics of trusses well. Rectangular cross-sections can be useful for broad, heavily loaded structures such as railway bridges. Pentagonal and circular structures give a very characterful form popular for enclosed footbridges, usually preferable to rectangular forms for this use. However, they can look out of scale with traditional small-scaled architecture, and the junction with buildings must be very carefully handled (see also Chapter 12).

7.34a (above) St Katharine's Dock, London: multi-planar truss for gangway – classic simplicity.

7.35a (left) Spandau Bridge, Berlin: 3-D truss, minimizing apparent depth when viewed from river.

7.35b (left) Bridgewater Street Footbridge, Manchester: very heavy tubular truss.

7.36a (left) Pecos River Bridge, New Mexico. The colour loses the structure against the background when it should have been bold.

7.36b (right) Limehouse Cut, East London. The crisp white truss stands out from the background and the balustrade.

7.36c (below) Irene Hixon Whitney Bridge, Minneapolis, Minnesota. Colour plays down the approach ramps well, but the treatment of the main spans is fussy and unnecessary.

7.36 Colour schemes for painting trusses should emphasize the structural form and make a clear distinction between structure and ancillary items like balustrades, handrails, lighting columns, infill panels, etc. Diagonal and vertical truss members should generally not be painted a different colour from top and bottom booms. All visible faces of any particular member should generally be the same colour to avoid the structure looking two-dimensional. Bolts and bracing or fixing plates should not be picked out in a contrasting colour. Ancillary parts, especially balustrades, should not be coloured to be more dominant visually than the structure, i.e. they should be more neutral in colour. Historic bridges, however, should use the historically correct colour scheme (see also Chapter 21).

Chapter 8
Suspension bridges

8.1 When this form of design is adopted it is generally for very large spans, though it can be used with advantage for small ornamental bridges. *In all cases, the curved line of the cables is the arresting feature. Particular care is needed to make the most of the beauty of line.* Surveys showing that the public prefer curves in bridges mean that suspension bridges can be more beautiful to the layperson than cable-stayed bridges.

8.2 If the cables come down so near the deck at the centre as to be below the balustrade level, this may spoil the side elevation. The practice of exposing the anchorage cable below deck level is aesthetically unfortunate if there is a sudden change in direction.

8.3 Design of the pylons is a difficult problem. Early suspension bridges generally had massive twin pylons with an arch between; this was in harmony with the rather heavier design tradition of those days. A lighter appearance is now generally preferred (also for economic reasons) and can be achieved by fairly slender steel or concrete twin pylons with a minimum of bracing members. The treatment at the tops of the pylons also needs careful consideration as these are so conspicuous; non-functional ornamentation here is likely to appear unreal and out of place. Walkways at the tops of pylons need very careful handling.

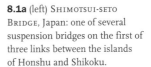

8.1a (left) SHIMOTSUI-SETO BRIDGE, Japan: one of several suspension bridges on the first of three links between the islands of Honshu and Shikoku.

8.2a (above) TAMAR BRIDGE, Saltash: note change of direction of cable.

8.1b (left, centre) MOUNT USHER GARDENS, Ashford, Co. Wicklow, Ireland: pedestrian suspension bridge.

8.3a (left) SÄÄKSMÄKI BRIDGE, Finland: simple treatment of pylons.

8.6a (left) Severn Bridge: aerodynamic deck section.

8.4a (below) Rossenstein Park Bridge, Stuttgart, Germany.

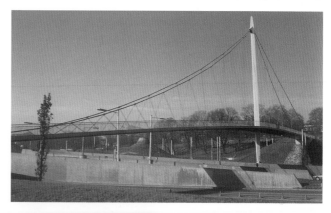

8.4b (left) Elx Bridge, Spain.

8.7a (below) Pont de la Fouvrière, Lyon, France.

8.4 Suspension bridges are generally symmetrical, though site considerations may occasionally dictate asymmetry. Asymmetrical bridges with pylons only at one end can have advantages.

8.5 Two lines of suspension cables are usual but there are examples of monocable designs, especially for footbridges. They tend to need diagonal hangers for structural reasons, which add to their elegance and emphasize their three-dimensional form.

8.6 Decks of large suspension bridges tend to be either trusses or aerodynamic sections, both of which can look elegant. Views out from the bridge and downward to the water below should be maintained for passengers in cars, coaches and trains. This can be helped by having pedestrian decks at a different level from the roadway (or railway on combined structures).

8.7 Occasionally, where topography and geology permit, the suspension cables can be rock anchored without masts, such as on the Pont de la Fouvrière, Lyon.

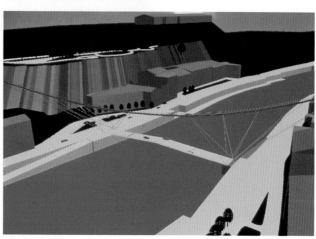

Chapter 9
Cable-stayed bridges

9.1 Bridge cables have a strong visual presence, which adds drama and can be used to produce very appealing bridges. *To be fully effective, however, the pattern of the cables must have clarity and unity.*

9.2 Clarity can be lost when a jumble of cables crossing at different angles is seen in an oblique view through two or more cable planes. There are several ways to resolve this problem:

● Use a single plane of cables.
● For two or more planes, adopt the harp configuration so that all cables on one side of a tower are parallel and never cross each other.
● With two planes in the fan configuration, tilt them inwards so that they touch at their apex. All the cables converge to a point and never cross. The effect is particularly dramatic when viewed from below. In practice, the requirements of the anchorages do not allow the cables to converge fully and the 'modified fan' is used, but the solution may still be effective.
● Use a myriad of small cables at close centres. The pattern is read as a pattern of planes, not of individual cables. The clashes become a moiré pattern, which can be beautiful. What number constitutes a myriad? This is a subjective question which can be answered by studying models, both physical and digital.

9.3 The unity of the cable pattern depends on the gradual progression of cable spacings and, when the 'planes' are not plane, on the smooth development of the warped geometry.

9.2a (above) BROTONNE BRIDGE, River Seine, Le Harve. A single plane of cables is the best solution for clarity.

9.2d (right) ANNACIS BRIDGE, British Columbia: a myriad of small cables at close centres.

9.2c (above) ST NAZAIRE BRIDGE, France: 'inclined fan' configuration – ugly relationship between piers and pylons.

9.2b (top) KESSOCK BRIDGE, Inverness: a striking oblique view of parallel cables.

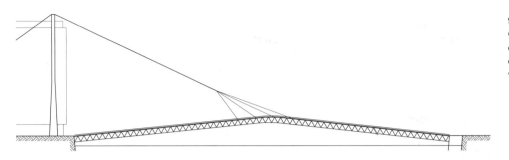

9.4a (left) THAMES FOOTBRIDGE, Coin Street, London. This unbuilt design is an extreme example of a cable arrangement dictated by the vertical alignment.

9.6a (right) ALL-PLASTICS ABERFELDY FOOTBRIDGE, Scotland. The towers are strong, simple, single elements, with no visually distracting crossbeams above the roadway.

9.6c (below) PONT D'ISÈRE, France: a successful expanded top anchorage to a mast.

9.6b (above) KNIEBRÜCKE BRIDGE, Düsseldorf. Classic simplicity of masts and cables.

9.4 Sometimes it is important to consider the relationship of the cable geometry to the vertical alignment of the deck. This will often have long approaches on a straight grade joined by a vertical curve across the main span. It can be very effective if the ends of the curve are positioned at the end cable anchorages on the deck so that the alignment appears to bend itself against the support of the cables.

9.5 The strength and clarity of the cable arrangement should be matched by similar attributes in the deck and towers. The deck usually should appear slender, but care is needed to

ensure that the cable anchorages do not disrupt its visual flow, either in elevation or in oblique views from below. It is wrong to make the anchorages invisible, but they should not be dominant. The anchorages should express their function of transferring the load, and should not be hidden in a box.

9.6 If possible, the tower should be seen rising from the ground (or water) to the top as a single element, unless the bridge is an opening type which can visually break at the pivot point. Here slenderness is not necessarily the goal. Indeed, a stronger visual line may improve the appearance.

Again, the cable anchorages must not disturb the flow and it is usually possible to contain them within the towers. The top anchorage to the mast should be as neat as possible. Expanded heads are seldom visually successful.

9.7 Any crossbeams between the legs of the tower detract from the visual simplicity. This is particularly true for crossbeams above the roadway, which destroy the dramatic clear slot to the sky. If crossbeams are proposed, the free-standing alternative with larger verticals should also be considered. The grandfather of this alternative is the Kniebrücke, which crosses the Rhine at Düsseldorf. Technically, the solution is well matched to the harp configuration adopted here because much of the load onto the tower is applied near the bottom, allowing a striking slenderness in the legs. The slenderness, both actual and apparent, can also be emphasized by tapering the towers over their full height.

9.8 The success of the design depends on the selection of span arrangement, cable pattern and tower form being well matched to suit the requirements of the site and each other. A study of successful designs will show what is possible. The greatest clarity of form is achieved with a single, central stay plane as at Brotonne (see Fig. 9.2a) and Tampa Bay (see Fig. 14.5b). A particularly successful example is the Farø Bridge where the central plane is lightly held between twin, inclined legs. Removed from the constriction of the central reservation, the legs can be slightly bolder in their dimensions and make a better foil for the delicate cables.

9.9 There are several constructional and economic reasons which prompt designers to adopt twin-stay planes which support the decks along their edges. However, the economic deck form for their approach viaducts is usually centrally supported with a spine structure, so there is a mismatch at the join. This can be resolved by a major support structure which also acts as a punctuation mark to celebrate the start of the main part of the bridge. The problem can be neatly avoided when the edge-supported deckform is carried into the approaches. It would be good to see the logic taken the other way, using the economics of the centrally supported approaches to prompt the use of a single-plane main span.

9.8a (left) Poole Bridge Competition Design, Dorset. A single carriageway with a single plane of cables requires a curved deck and a leaning mast.

9.8b (below) Farø Bridge, Denmark: single plane of cables between two inclined legs.

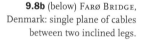

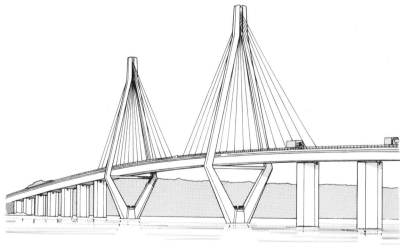

9.9a (left) Queen Elizabeth II Bridge, Dartford: a bad mismatch between supports for the approach viaducts and the main span.

9.10 Where the bridge is curved in plan, the cables can be encased in concrete as in the Ganter Bridge, or fan out to rock anchorages as in the Ruck-a-Chucky Bridge design. There is an S-shaped bridge in Tokyo. These can give rise to some very unusual and dynamic forms.

9.11 If the deck structure is a triangulated truss, the directions of the truss members should be co-ordinated with those of the cables. This is most easily achieved with a harp configuration for the cables as in the two-level alternative for the Øresund Crossing.

9.12 Most designers will not have the opportunity to design major, long-span bridges, but there are frequent situations where a cable-stayed configuration is appropriate for footbridges. When planning pedestrian routes, it is important to remember that pedestrians need to know where to go. A footbridge pylon rising above the urban clutter is a clear goal. There are factors, however, which often make cable-stayed footbridges less elegant than their long-span cousins. If they are understood, they can be addressed.

9.13 The visual depth of the deck is generally dominated by the height of the parapet, which is usually much more than the structural depth needed. The appearance suffers as a result. This is compounded if the deck structure is placed below the walkway. One response is to use a visually light parapet, possible with tensioned wires, so the visual depth is read as that of the structure.

9.10a (left) GANTER BRIDGE, Switzerland: concrete-encased cables in a dramatic structured form.

9.10b (below) RUCK-A-CHUCKY BRIDGE, USA: unbuilt proposal.

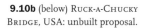

9.13a (left) PASSERELLE PAS DU LAC, St Quentin-en-Yvelines, France. Deck structure below walkway increases overall depth and visual weight.

9.11a (left) ØRESUND CROSSING: trussed, two-level central span, road above, rail beneath.

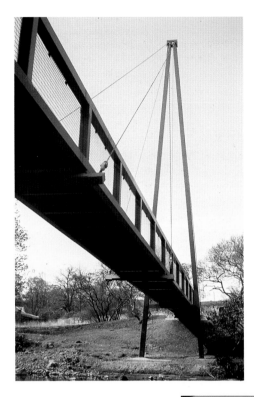

9.14a (left) ALMOND VALLEY
FOOTBRIDGE, Lothian:
heavy vertical members
of vierendeel truss.

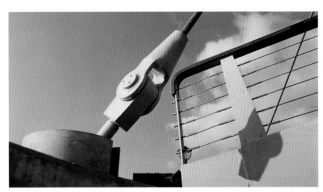

9.15b (left)
RIVER AIRE
FOOTBRIDGE,
Leeds:
tensioned
wires used
for parapet.

9.15a (right) RIVER AIRE
FOOTBRIDGE, Leeds: main deck
booms at pedestrians' calf height.

9.14 A 'half-through' deck can be used, with a truss structure doubling up as the parapet. This reduces the depth but the diagonals detract from the essential horizontality of the deck. The alternative of vierendeel trusses is not generally successful because they need such heavy members.

9.15 A promising variation is where the main deck booms are RHS tubes outside the parapet at calf height to the pedestrians. Visual lightness is achieved with a clear gap at ankle height, but there is structural interaction across the gap with discrete sheer transfer elements.

9.16 The anchorage details are often proportionately larger than on big bridges, so particular care is needed with them. This is compounded by the frequent use of inclined cable planes. If the anchorage is at footplate level then it has to be held out so that the cable clears the parapet rail. The main structure can be moved out towards the cable plane and the anchor level raised so that they are not seen in oblique views from below.

PICTURE CREDITS
9.2a d Campenon Bernard; ph Jean Muller. **9.2b d** Dr Helmut Homberg; ph Harry Sowden. **9.2c** ph Magnum/Bruno Barbey. **9.2d d**/ph Buckland & Taylor Ltd. **9.4a d** Arup. **9.6a d**/ph Maunsell Structural Plastics. **9.6b d** Fritz Leonhardt; ph Robert Harding Picture Library/Graham Turnill. **9.6c d**/ph Jean Muller/Alain Spielmann. **9.8a d** Norman Foster/Arup. **9.8b** illus Fred English. **9.9a d** Dartford River Crossing Ltd; ph JW. **9.10a d** Christian Menn; ph M Darbellay-Martigny. **9.10b d**/ph TY Lin International. **9.11a d**/ph Arup. **9.13a d** Alain Spielmann. **9.14a d**/ph Arup. **9.15a d** Arup; ph Paul White Photography. **9.15b d** Arup; ph Paul White Photography.

Chapter 10
Mixed-form bridges

10.1 Different structural forms may be incorporated into one bridge. This can either be sequential, where a series of bridges is linked together as on two of Japan's Honshu-Shikoku crossings, or in an integrated structure where the load is taken jointly by different forms of structure acting in unison, such as Robert Maillart's deck-stiffened arch at Valtschiel (Fig. 4.14b).

10.2 The most common is the sequential form. This may occur, for example, where a long viaduct crosses a moderately wide river. In such a case the physical problem will generally dictate the character of the main bridge, and the approaches will differ in scale and form, often contrasting with the main structure. With narrower crossings the main span may well harmonize with the viaduct approaches, preserving a common character throughout. *In this matter, as in most others where there are aesthetic considerations, vagueness, indecision and weak compromise are the cardinal sins.*

10.3 It is important to keep elements which recur in the sequential structures similar to each other. For instance, the deck structure and depth should be constant for the main span and approach spans (not as in the River Adda Bridge), and the form of piers should stay constant, unlike the Queen Elizabeth II Bridge at Dartford (see Fig. 9.9a).

10.1a (below) THE FIRST HONSHU-SHIKOKU LINK, Japan: beam bridges, a trussed viaduct, two cable-stayed and one suspension bridge.

10.1b (above) EAST LONDON RIVER CROSSING: proposed design by Santiago Calatrava. Truss and cantilever structure are expertly combined.

10.3a (right) RIVER ADDA BRIDGE, Lombardy, Italy: trussed approach spans incompatible with main arch.

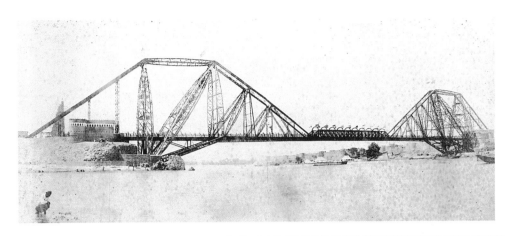

10.4a (left) LANSDOWNE BRIDGE, River Indus, Pakistan: the most unsightly bridge in the world? No consistency of angle or scale, nor any clarity of form.

10.5a (below) OLGASTRASSE FOOTBRIDGE, Zürich, Switzerland.

10.4 Where different structural forms act in unison, the whole bridge should be designed as one integrated structure, not like the now-demolished Lansdowne Bridge in Pakistan, which combined different truss configurations in a clumsy cantilever structure – claimed as the most unsightly in the world.

10.5 Where the deck acts as a beam which works compositely with an arch, the resultant light and delicate trussed arch structure should be exploited. Examples are ABK's design for a new bridge alongside the existing Lutyens and Arup bridges at Runnymede (Fig. 25.8a), or Santiago Calatrava's Oberbaum Bridge (Fig. 7.2e).

PICTURE CREDITS
10.1a ph Orion Press **10.1b d**/ph Santiago Calatrava. **10.3a** ph Italcementi. **10.4a** ph Guinness Book of Structures. **10.5a d** Santiago Calatrava; ph JW.

Chapter 11
Broad highway bridges

11.1 Broad underbridges and viaducts with a breadth to carry in excess of a dual three-lane road have particular problems with regard to the space below them. They used to be very rare but are likely to become increasingly common, especially with widened motorways and additional slip roads (see also Chapter 27).

11.2 Little light and no rain penetrate under broad bridges; the space tends to have hard finishes or be bare earth, and is dark and forbidding to pedestrians. It tends to attract graffiti, rubbish and vagrants, which exacerbate the situation.

11.3 Where possible, underbridges in such situations should be avoided (see Chapter 2, Paragraph 2.15).

11.4 The difficulties can be handled in different ways depending on whether the bridge is short-span, long-span or multi-span, or over a river.

11.5 *Short-span bridges will be considerably shorter than their breadth, making in effect a tunnel. The length of the tunnel is increased when the road or path using it also passes under amenity bunds beside the main road. Such bridges should in principle be treated as tunnels (see Chapter 17) whose length* should be minimized by not taking bunds over the minor road, by reducing skew where possible and avoiding a deck structure solely for the purpose of sightlines on a bend. The apparent tunnel length should also be reduced in length by visual effects where possible, e.g. by widening entrances vertically and horizontally in plan to give an apparent shortening, and cantilevering the deck beyond the walls at the entrances. The interior should be lit in the daytime. Over-spanning has little visual advantage except to give a sloping hard wall, which is less prone to graffiti. The elevation of the bridge should be treated as a tunnel portal.

11.6 *Long-span and multi-span bridges have a scale which is extremely difficult to integrate into the landscape, so the breadth should be actually and apparently reduced as much as possible.* The higher the clearance and the longer the span, the less the breadth will be apparent. Long-edge cantilevers give

11.5a (below) RIVER WINIFRED BRIDGE, A35 Chideock Bypass, Dorset: suggested proposal. A 10m high parabolic arch allows the maximum natural light into the 40m long river and pedestrian underpass.

11.6a (right) BISHOPTHORPE BRIDGE, York: long-edge cantilevers and excellent modelling.

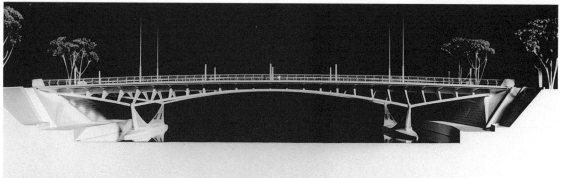

11.6b (left) KRONPRINZEN BRIDGE, Berlin. Expressive structure relieves oppressive soffit.

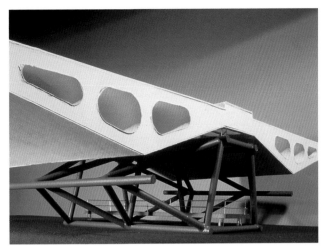

11.6d (left) ALSOP AND STÖRMER PROTOTYPE: bridge with pedestrian deck below to minimize width.

11.6c (above) UNIVERSITY OF CALABRIA, Italy. Underslung pedestrian deck narrows actual width.

11.6e (left) ST GOTTHARD VIADUCT, Switzerland. Split decks minimize visual intrusion of broad deck.

11.6f (right) BIASCA BRIDGE, Switzerland. Splitting the carriageways and emphasizing the height makes the deck seem narrow.

11.6g (right) OVER BRIDGE, A40 Gloucester Bypass. Light penetrates further with a long cantilever.

less breadth of structure under the bridge and allow more light and rain to penetrate, extending planting further under the bridge. The soffit will be visually very dominant, therefore it should be modelled to emphasize the span direction. This can be done by curving it or by expressing the structure as on Waterloo Bridge, London (Fig. 5.3b). Expressive structures also relieve the oppressiveness of the soffit. The width can be physically narrowed as well as visually relieved by placing a pedestrian deck in a truss below the main deck. Separating carriageways significantly improves the appearance but must be detailed safely.

11.7 *Broad bridges over water can be especially unpleasant for boaters and walkers, and particular effort should be made to relieve the inherent problems.* Bridges over water offer the potential of its reflecting quality to relieve the darkness under broad bridges, by increasing actual light levels and by giving a moving dappled effect on the soffit.

This advice should be taken together with the comments in Paragraph 11.6 above. Separating carriageways to permit light to penetrate under the bridge is potentially important, since with water's reflective properties, the visual effect of the light penetration is quadrupled by reflection and dispersal. Even a relatively narrow slot of light is of great benefit, especially in

11.7a (left) M25 RUNNYMEDE
BRIDGES: gap between the Lutyens
and Arup bridges to lighten
pedestrian route.

rural situations. A high gloss or white finish to the substructure has been found to help reflected light penetration. Where the watercourse is narrow in proportion to the bridge span, the possibility of widening it, even to creating a lake or exploiting balancing ponds, should be considered. This can help the setting of the bridge, avoid difficult-to-use hard spaces under the bridge, improve the landscaping and possibly add benefits to the community, such as watersports. In urban situations, the space under the bridge including the abutments should be treated in an urban way as townscape, incorporating stairs, viewing platforms, shops, cafés and mooring facilities, etc., appropriate to its urban

setting, as under Waterloo Bridge on London's South Bank (Fig. 27.6c). The possibility of incorporating buildings should be considered in side spans, like the National Film Theatre at the same location (see Chapter 27). As with all urban bridges, the relationship to adjacent architecture is very important (see also Chapter 14).

PICTURE CREDITS
11.5a d Rust; illus Fred English. **11.6a d** Arup. **11.6b d**/ph Santiago Calatrava. **11.6c d** Vittorio Gregotti. **11.6d d** Alsop and Störmer. **11.6e d** Christian Menn; ph JW. **11.6f d** Christian Menn; ph JW. **11.6g** ph JW. **11.7a d** Lutyens/Arup; ph JW.

Chapter 12

Footbridges

12.1 The light loading associated with footbridges provides opportunities for slender, elegant design. Their relatively low cost on multi-bridge schemes makes them particularly suitable for enhancement on motorways where something dramatic is needed to contrast with the generally low-key structures (see Chapter 2, Paragraph 2.3) for enhanced driver alertness and awareness of location. Unusual forms of construction are particularly appropriate where long spans are dictated by the need to avoid the excessive structural implications of collision resistance on columns and decks of footbridges. *Footbridges, therefore, should be slender, elegant, dramatic and unusual* (see Fig. 2.3a).

12.2 Since footbridges are used at a slow pace by pedestrians, quality of detail and of surface texture are important.

12.3 Since the pedestrian experience of the bridge relates to the surrounding environment, and not generally to the road, *the bridge and particularly its approaches should relate to the adjacent environment from the pedestrian's point of view.* This is particularly so in rural areas and where a more urban road severs a public open space or woodland.

12.4 The precise location of footbridges is more adjustable than most bridges, and the advice in Chapter 2 is therefore relevant at the later stages of scheme design for footbridges.

12.5 A footbridge should be positioned for optimum use. The route of its main span, steps and ramps should follow the desire line as much as possible, though privacy of local residents must not be compromised.

12.6 *It is important for pedestrians to see where they are heading, and to have no hidden corners which might give a fear of or threat from muggers.* Bridge spans should therefore be straight, especially where through girders or trusses are used.

Where the pedestrian route is long and not simple or straight, for instance across multiple traffic corridors (road, rail, canal), it is important to have a major visual feature or marker so that people can see where they are going and where the route leads. The masts of cable-stayed bridges and other such bold and dramatic structures are particularly good for this (see Fig. 2.20a).

ACCESS

12.7 *Ramps are often the most ugly and environmentally damaging part of a pedestrian bridge and should be avoided or minimized wherever possible,* though with due regard for need by the disabled and those with prams. Utilizing the local topography is the best means for minimization.

12.8 If an at-grade crossing is located at a distance from the bridge such that to use it would be less than twice the length of the ramps and main span, then the ramps to the bridge are unnecessary as they will not be used in preference to the at-grade crossing.

12.7a (above) A316, Hanworth, West London: hideous and overbearing pedestrian ramps. A ramp and steps on a bund would have been better.

12.2a (left) JAPAN BRIDGE, La Défense, Paris. Quality of detail is important for footbridges.

12.9a (left) Passerelle Pas Du Lac, St Quentin-en-Yvelines, France: ramp and steps built into bund (see also 9.13a).

12.12a (right) A27 Brighton Bypass, East Sussex: an elegant footbridge exploiting the contours well.

12.9 Steps and ramps, if necessary, should be built into the ground, utilizing bunds where possible, since this gives more route options (i.e. short cuts) and less distance enclosed by structure (which can generate fear of being trapped by muggers). Steps and ramps should be as near as possible on the desire line, to avoid short cuts damaging planting.

12.10 For the infirm and others who need to use them, ramps should preferably be at a slope of 1:20, and landings are not then required. Unfortunately, this is what leads to their visual and environmental intrusiveness. A balance needs to be made between their usefulness and their environmental damage in each particular situation, and the design fine-tuned. Ramps up to 1:12 are acceptable with landings, and where 1:20 is not practical. Steeper ramps are only acceptable under certain conditions, e.g. where the approach path is steeper than 1:12, where the ramp would chase the contours and not reach the ground, or where the ramp would require the loss of mature trees, particularly in ancient woodland. Stepped ramps can be a useful compromise in these situations.

12.11 No ramps are necessary where the terrain on the access to the footbridge is such that it is inaccessible to those needing ramps and there are no proposals to improve the approaches, e.g. because it is in the countryside, because it is in ancient woodland, or because there are steps or rocks on the approach. No ramps should be provided when environmental damage from their construction is greater than the benefit to the disabled and pram users, as when usage is low or the bridge is approached across seasonally boggy terrain.

12.12 When a footbridge is in cutting or false cutting, the bridge should span to the top or face of the cutting, not stop short of it with steps or ramps on the structure, even if the footpath is at the lower level. In such cases the steps or ramps should either be constructed within the face of the cutting, or preferably the path should link down along the top or other contours of the bund or cutting to meet a redirected footpath. Footpaths are best redirected at some distance from a new road, not redirected alongside it until the crossing point is reached. This should be exploited for footbridge approaches (see also Chapter 2, Paragraphs 2.10–2.11).

12.13 A simple way to visually lose the steps and ramps of a footbridge is to put them beyond an existing hedgerow or tree line. This conceals them from the road and masks vehicles from pedestrians. A slight additional span length may be necessary, as may some extra land, which should be allowed for.

12.14 Where the approaches are from a lower level, it is important to keep the steps or ramps as light as possible, particularly when both are required. Effective designs have been achieved when the approach steps and footbridge itself form a single structure. Full use should be made of camber to achieve headroom and reduce approach steps or ramps.

12.15 The lowest 1m–1.5m height of ramp is best put on a bund, preferably contoured into adjacent landscaping. Where this is not possible the ramp should preferably be supported on walls to avoid rubbish collecting below.

12.16 The structural form and scale of the ramp spans should relate to those of the main span. Where the latter is large and delicate, such as a through truss, the ramp should have a balustrade height-to-span ratio similar to the truss height-to-span ratio of the main span. This is valid where the ramp structure is a through truss or a shallow-beam deck (see Chapter 7). Where the main span is a simple steel, concrete or composite beam, the ramp spans should look similar and have a similar depth-to-span ratio as the main span. Where the main span is of more unusual form, such as cable-stay or bowstring arch, the ramp structure should not follow that form.

12.17 Due to the small size of ramp structures, columns are generally best used singly, and if there is need for a crosshead, it is best integral with the deck structure or the deck's supporting beams. Trussed or braced ramp support structures in steel or concrete with two or four posts are best avoided, since they are fussy, clutter the roadside and look temporary. Such supports in timber construction may be necessary due to the nature of the material, and are then best kept as simple as possible and preferably in one plane.

12.18 Ramps should have as simple a geometry as possible, ideally a single straight run on the desire line. When the ramp is along the approach path on the desire line, and there is no other approach, then steps are not required in addition. Ramps curved in plan can be more visually pleasing and less mechanical, but should be related to site features. When ramps are curved, there should preferably be a continuous flowing line in elevation, not broken by landings, and this should be continuous with the line of the main span deck in elevation. A cambered main span can assist this flowing line.

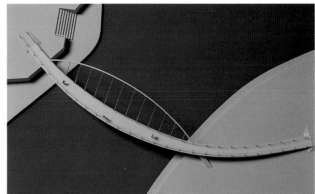

12.16a (above) MERCHANT BRIDGE, Manchester. Simple approach span complements bold main span.

12.18a (right) WISLEY FOOTBRIDGE, A3, Surrey. The approach ramp should join the main span smoothly in plan and elevation.

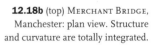

12.18b (top) MERCHANT BRIDGE, Manchester: plan view. Structure and curvature are totally integrated.

12.18c (left) FOOTBRIDGE, Kuwait: flowing curvature.

12.19 Spiral ramps can look very elegant with their strong geometric form and graceful curves acting as a natural continuation of the deck. Large radii are generally visually more delicate and airy than tight radii. Stacked spiral ramps tend to lose the elegance of the form, and free-form or S-shaped ramps are to be preferred. The circular spiral ramp is usually too harsh and geometric for rural areas, where a free form is more appropriate if curved ramps are proposed.

12.20 Straight folded and stacked ramps are particularly unpleasant, especially where the runs are short and the balustrades tall, since this gives the appearance of a large cage, particularly when the balustrade almost reaches the soffit of the ramp-over. Not only does it look unpleasant, but the public are unlikely to want to use it.

12.21 *Steps to footbridges can be difficult to make elegant, but they are smaller than ramps for the same rise.* A single flight along the desire line is a good solution, but can look very lumpen if the bridge is banana-shaped. Steps can also be built into the legs of sloping supports to form an elegant and logical design. Symmetry within a flight is often a good solution, with flights splitting, folding and radiating, and landings turned into viewing platforms and passing places. Much can be learnt from Baroque garden layout, and particularly staircase geometry, but interpreted usually in a more modern way. Walls, alcoves and terraces can be exploited to give a more urban form, especially where there is a natural change, or retaining walls. This is particularly useful where pedestrians use a larger bridge (e.g. a high-level river bridge or viaduct) and then need to return down to a lower level.

12.19a (top) A316, Hanworth, London: elegant spiral ramp, though piers could have been more slender.

12.21a (above) STADELHOFEN STATION, Zürich: steps symmetrically split and folded.

12.21b (above) OLGASTRASSE FOOTBRIDGE, Zürich: alcove exploited well (see also 10.5a).

12.22a (left) Southwark Bridge, London: pedestrian access to bridge unclear.

12.23a (below) Poplar Station, Docklands Light Railway, London: stairs and lift for access.

12.22b (below) London Bridge, Upper Thames Street steps: attractive only to muggers.

12.23c (bottom, left) Corniche, Jeddah, Saudi Arabia: bridge travolator.

12.23b (below) Waterloo Underpass, London: lift.

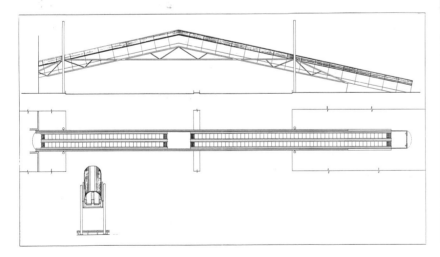

12.22 Steps incorporated within buildings or completely surrounded by walls are less satisfactory. This is because people cannot be seen in them, so they attract vandals, muggers and vagrants who use them as toilets. They therefore need more cleaning, look unpleasant and people are thus deterred from using them. Such steps must not be locked closed at any time, especially where a cul-de-sac would thus be formed to trap people, since this exacerbates the problem. Where steps are within buildings the entrance to them and the place where they are leading should be very visible and obvious by design, ideally obviating the need for signs.

12.23 Escalators, travolators and lifts should generally be enclosed to ease maintenance and keep them operative more of the time. The particular geometry of the mechanisms will dictate the form of the structure and enclosure. Since, inevitably, this will become a building fundamentally, especially where it is part of an enclosed bridge, an architect may well be needed for detailed design. Escalators have higher capacity than stairs (useful near rail termini) and can form a bridge in themselves. Lifts can take up less space than ramps, especially where the height is considerable.

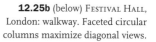

12.25a (left) FOOTBRIDGE, La Défense, Paris: slender, tapered leaf piers on elegant, curving bridge.

12.25b (below) FESTIVAL HALL, London: walkway. Faceted circular columns maximize diagonal views.

12.27a (above) MOSQUE FOOTBRIDGE, Jeddah. External columns separate from truss structure.

12.27b (right) BASINGSTOKE FOOTBRIDGE: unusual structure above deck.

STRUCTURE

12.24 Supports for main spans generally consist of columns and/or abutments. Chapter 6 covers the general situation, but footbridges have particular problems which need addressing.

12.25 The vehicle impact load required to be resisted by footbridge columns within 4.5m of the kerb makes them very large in proportion to the light structure possible with the light loading of the deck. A diameter 1.2m to 1.5m is common. Columns should never be broader than the deck or thicker than the deck structure. Slender leaf piers and columns tapered to give a stouter base can give elegant results in scale with the deck. Circular columns are generally better than square since they appear more slender on diagonal views. More refined shapes such as elliptical or lens-shaped, possibly also tapering, can be appropriate and elegant.

12.26 It is often better to span clear over the road, keeping all support structures 4.5m clear of the kerbs. (This also has constructional advantages on live roads and widened motorways.) Spans can then be large, often approaching 100m, which dictates substantial abutment structures. Visually these should appear robust enough for their purpose.

12.27 Trusses landing on light-braced steel towers can look very out-of-scale and awkward. Concrete or masonry can look more appropriate, and can form a suitable strongly defined break between the main span structure and the lighter ramp structure. To emphasize this function it can sometimes be appropriate for the abutment to extend above the deck or even above the balustrade, which can also visually simplify ramp, stair and main span junctions. Where columns or masts support the structure, they are better as pairs or singles, and can look excellent when extended above the truss and when the truss passes beyond the mast. In such situations the columns are best kept clear of the face of the truss and not appearing to be an extended member of the truss.

12.28 Simple beam bridges also tend to be improved by a heavy abutment structure to mark the transition from main span to ramp and stair structure. The exception is when the structure can continue visually at a similar depth, e.g. when a variable-depth beam is used for the main span, or when a slender box beam with long cantilevers is used.

12.29 Cable-stayed and suspension bridges have particular pier requirements which can be dramatized. Cantilever bridges have back spans which can be utilized for ramps and need low-key support columns.

12.30 Where a footbridge is part of a multi-level complex road interchange, it is better to treat the footbridge as an independent structure with its own form and geometry rather than as subservient to the main structure, e.g. hung off the flyover, since this can be very oppressive for the pedestrians.

SIGNS AND LIGHTING

12.31 Where gantry signs are needed close to footbridges, combining them can make for less environmental clutter (see also Chapters 24 and 25). But it is very important to do this at the earliest design stage, not as an afterthought: the two must be fully integrated. The scope for adjusting positions of footbridges makes them more suitable than many road bridges for combining with gantries. Since the plane of the sign relative to the road is fixed, the footbridge must follow this line, otherwise the sign will be offset at an awkward and ugly angle to the bridge.

12.32 Lighting of footbridges is generally best using the road lighting or low-level illumination incorporated in the handrail, parapet or floor. On structures which have high-level elements such as through trusses or cable-stayed structures, the lighting can successfully be integrated overhead, possibly utilizing masts for high mast lighting. Lighting columns along

12.29a (right) ST ANNE'S LAKE, Thorpe, Surrey. Ramped, cantilevered construction gives boat clearance logically.

12.30a (below) MARSH MILLS FOOTBRIDGE, Plymouth: independent of adjacent interchange.

12.32a (above) M6, Cheshire. An elegant footbridge lit by road lights.

12.32b (left) BELLS BRIDGE, Glasgow: excellent lighting.

a bridge are rarely successful unless specially designed with the bridge architecture (see Chapter 22).

MATERIALS

12.33 Parapets should generally be as light in form as possible and not confused with structure, e.g. with through trusses. Colour can help in this (see Chapter 21). Wherever practicable, solid parapets should be avoided. Timber is a particularly suitable material for pedestrian parapets, especially in rural areas since it 'feels' nice.

12.34 Main spans can be in any form of construction described in this book, and probably others besides. Likewise, materials can be anything herein described, though certain materials such as timber and plastics may be only mainly appropriate to footbridges (see Fig. 9.6a). The materials of any ramps or stairs should generally be similar to those of the main span, but mixing of materials can be an advantage. Steel beams with timber parapets can be particularly successful and appropriate for footbridges.

NON-ROAD FOOTBRIDGES

12.35 Non-road footbridges are primarily those built to divert footpaths over watercourses or rivers due to new roads or bridge widening. *They do not need to comply with highway requirements, and should generally be as simple as possible;* often a plank plus a handrail is perfectly adequate. A stile may also be needed in rural areas, where the watercourse follows a field boundary. Such bridges may also be incorporated with weirs. With modern lifting equipment, simple stone clapper bridges may be eminently suitable in areas where suitable freestone slabs are available, perhaps as quarry waste. In parkland settings, more unusual and exotic bridges can be appropriate to enhance the environment, and the collaboration of artists has produced some interesting examples. In general all such bridges should be quite rustic in appearance.

12.33a (above) FOOTBRIDGE, University of East Anglia. Structural glass parapets give the lightest appearance.

12.35c (right) ISOLE DEI PESCATORI, Lake Maggiore, Italy: an elegant modern steel footbridge.

12.34a (top) ESKDALE FOOTBRIDGE, Cumbria: timber parapet on a weathering steel structure.

12.35a (centre, left) RUNNYMEDE FOOTBRIDGE, Surrey. Non-road footbridges in busy areas may need a third rail or even mesh infill, depending on location.

12.35b (above) RIVER NADDER, Salisbury, Wiltshire. This simple footbridge is appropriate to its setting but in need of repair. Remote or low-risk bridges only need a handrail on one side.

12.35d (left) BOWSTRING FOOTBRIDGE: a simple and dynamic artist-designed structure in oak and stainless steel.

12.35e (above) FOOTBRIDGE, Vietnam. A plank, plus single handrail, is suitable for very short spans only; this is too fragile.

12.37b (left) HAYS WHARF, River Thames, London. The cladding on this footbridge to a pontoon does not follow the truss structure.

12.37a (above, centre) WATERLOO EAST LINK, London: a slick skin.

12.37c (above) FOOTBRIDGE, Jeddah, Saudi Arabia: laser-cut ornamental steel diaphragms acting as parapets.

12.37d (right) JAPAN BRIDGE, La Défense, Paris: maintenance gantry.

COVERED BRIDGES

12.36 Covered bridges have been used as architectural features for many centuries, e.g. the Bridge of Sighs in Venice. Due to the architectonic nature of the form and the requirements in the detailed design, it is usually best to involve an architect, particularly for the concept and for the detailed design of the cladding. There are two basic approaches: (a) a through truss, where the structure directly supports the cladding walls and roof, and (b) a deck structure, off which a light frame supports the cladding to walls and roof.

12.37 Through trusses are covered in Chapter 7 (note Paragraph 7.35 particularly). The cladding can either be external or internal to the structure. External cladding can give a smooth slick skin, and this should be the aim. Mullions, transoms and any secondary structure should be minimized, and in particular should not appear to be main structure. This approach can give easy access for structural maintenance. A slick skin needs regular cleaning to keep it looking good, and facilities for this should be allowed for in the design. Placing the cladding inside the structure allows the structure to be expressed rather than hidden, and simplifies cladding

12.37e (right) Pons Russien, Switzerland: traditional covered timber bridge.

12.39a (below) Riyadh University Footbridge, Saudi Arabia: slick tube on a light trussed, cable-supported cradle – complexity with clarity.

12.38a (above) St Olaf Wharf Footbridge, London. Light glazing over a through girder or beam gives a neat and simple design.

12.39b (bottom left) Duke's Hill Footbridge, London. Heavy deck masks ramped walkway.

12.39c (below) Bracknell Ring Road Footbridge, Berkshire. The fussy cladding conflicts with the simple structure.

installation, which can be useful over live roads. External access by vandals can be a problem. The mullions and transoms and any sub-frame should follow the same geometry as the structure, though need not follow every member. Additional glazing members not following structural members should be avoided. Infill panels within the voids of the truss on the same plane should be avoided, since the constructional tolerances and movement of civil engineering structures are much larger than for architectural cladding, thus requiring very large and obtrusive movement joints. The exception is where steel panels, either plain or perforated, are welded to the structure to act as a diaphragm. The possibility of distortion and deformation should be allowed for. Timber boarding or shingles have traditionally been fixed direct to timber, since it can tolerate large movement.

12.38 Through trusses when clad need to be approximately 3m high; this often exceeds purely structural needs and can look very cumbersome. A useful compromise is the half-through girder or truss, where the deck is supported off the bottom flange of a beam about 1.5m high, giving structure up to handrail height, and then a glazed barrel vault.

12.39 Cladding supported off deck structure visually separates deck from cladding, and permits slender decks and less heavy parapets. This is appropriate to concrete structures, simple beam structures and suspended structures, e.g. cable-stayed. The horizontal split of the elevation can help the bridge appear more slender and dynamic. The structure usually should appear to be a third or less of the overall height of the structure plus cladding. An edge cantilever can help the proportions.

12.40 Cladding wrapping round to include the roof, which can be curved or pitched, visually minimizes the height and avoids the need for eaves gutters. This is generally the best form. The structure need not be exposed, but this gives a strange 'spacecraft' feel, which can be exciting, especially seen against buildings, but it is not appropriate everywhere.

12.41 Where ramps, escalators and stairs are clad, unless there is a linear run, all the elements should be within a greater enclosure, with space around them. They should not be clad individually, since this gives a cumbersome, overcomplex, unwelcoming and fussy design.

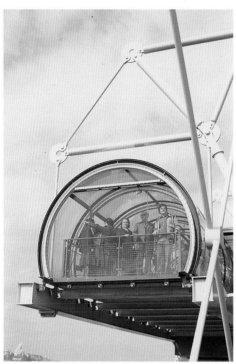

12.40a (right) CENTRE POMPIDOU, Paris: simple glazed tube on hoops.

12.40b (top) BRIDGE AT POPLAR, Docklands Light Railway: sophisticated tube split for ventilation.

12.41a (above) A62, Manchester Street, Oldham, Lancashire: how not to clad a bridge and its ramps.

12.40c (left) JAPAN BRIDGE, La Défense, Paris. Section need not be circular or rectangular.

12.42a (left) Hays Wharf Footbridge, London: simple glass cladding to elegant truss.

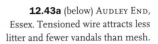

12.43a (below) Audley End, Essex. Tensioned wire attracts less litter and fewer vandals than mesh.

12.42 For glazing, a clear, tough, scratch resistant, non-yellowing, easily cleanable material which breaks safely is required. Toughened laminated glass or laminates with glass outer layers are best. Where sheets need to be bent for curved glazing, acrylic has been found to be the best of the plastics materials, though, as with all plastics, it has poor scratch resistance, especially during graffiti removal.

12.43 Where cladding is only needed to stop objects being thrown from a bridge, a fine stainless steel zoo mesh or closely spaced tensioned wires are best. Coarse-welded concrete reinforcing mesh or diagonal-woven fencing meshes are generally inappropriate and prison-like – a challenge to vandals rather than a discouragement, as well as looking unpleasant. Flat mesh roofs are particularly untidy, collect rubbish and permit easy vandal access. Barrel-vaulted garden pergola type structures with tensioned wires or fine metal strapwork do not have the same negative connotations and are difficult to walk on.

Chapter 13

Railway bridges

13.1 For functional reasons, bridges carrying railways differ in several characteristic ways from those carrying roads. There is no need to disguise these differences in the interest of uniformity. A railway bridge over a road should be easily recognized as such.

13.2 Differences arise for a number of reasons:

- The loads are heavier and are carried on a narrow deck.
- Due to the specific loading characteristics of moving trains, railway bridges need to be stiffer than road bridges.

- Constraints on the vertical alignment of the railway are often severe, and through or half-through structures are often used to minimize the structural depth required below the rail. Traditionally these structures are steel with vertical webs. In concrete such structures can appear much lighter because the side surfaces can more easily be inclined.

13.3 On existing railways the constraints on the horizontal alignment, even for temporary periods, usually result in railway bridges being built off-line and placed during a weekend possession. This may result in a structure with a clear break or change in form at each end of the placed section. It is often best to express the break and to allow the placed section to express its own character.

13.2a (right) CROSSGATE VIADUCT, Tyne & Wear. Inclined concrete side surfaces mask the depth of the ballasted track.

13.1a (below) LUDGATE BRIDGE, London (now demolished): typical of innumerable nineteenth-century wrought iron railway bridges.

13.3a (left) G-MEX BRIDGE, Manchester Metrolink. The steel structure contrasts boldly with its surroundings.

13.4a (below) CROSSGATE VIADUCT, Tyne & Wear. The light, open parapet reinforces the slenderness of the deck and allows the bridge's function to be expressed vividly when a train passes across it.

13.5a (below) A20 RAIL BRIDGE, Newington. Acoustic barriers should not appear structural, especially where the structure itself is delicate, as here; also the power line masts clutter this bridge.

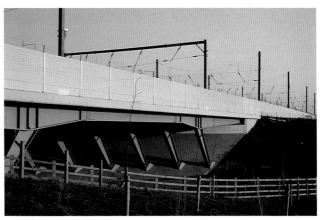

13.4 The parapet railings can be quite light and open.

13.5 Overhead electrification may be needed. On short bridges, up to 40m long, the posts should be kept off the bridge. On longer bridges, the supports for the posts should be integrated neatly with the structure and the other fittings of the bridge. Where a viaduct is particularly long or prominent, the option to place the masts between the tracks should be considered. For maintenance access, masts are usually placed on the outside of pairs of tracks, forming an intrusive avenue of clutter. With additional separation between the tracks and some safety fences for people working between the tracks, a single line of posts can be used.

13.6 On historic rail bridges the detail design and position of any alteration, such as power gantries and bridge bashing beams, is of great importance.

13.7 The sudden noise of a train on a bridge can be alarming and disruptive. The 'appearance' of a railway bridge in a wider sense includes its acoustic response, and the designer must ensure that this is appropriate to the local context. In peaceful surroundings it will be necessary to use a heavy form of construction, with some degree of containment above rail level.

13.8 The requirements for bridges which carry a road over a railway are similar to those for road over road. However, there are some additional considerations:
● Trains deposit a fine brown powder from their brake shoes on trackside structures. This powder is magnetic and thus

tends to stick. On the approaches to stations, therefore, the deposits can be heavy. All light finishes will be discoloured and the best defence is probably dark brown brick facings.
● Long abutment walls adjacent to a railway may require refuges where maintenance gangs can wait as trains pass. The need for these should be identified early in the design process so they can be accommodated in the basic strategy.

13.9 Where the road passes over the rail, abutment wingwalls are best parallel to the railway, since the speed and angle of view from the train make them less noticeable and the landscape is emphasized for other viewers.

13.10 Solid concrete parapets may be required for safety reasons over the bridge (Fig. 6.14a). They may be textured or clad in accordance with Department of Transport guidance. The weight of the solid parapet may limit the extent of edge cantilevers on the deck. It may be appropriate to consider moving the heavy parapet to the line of the edge of the carriageway and using normal steel or aluminium parapets at the edge of the deck. Where concrete parapets meet steel or aluminium, the concrete height can be sloped down to meet the metal parapet, giving continuity to the line.

13.11 Many of the principles referred to for highway bridges in Chapter 6 are also applicable to railway bridges.

PICTURE CREDITS
13.1a ph Arup. **13.2a d**/ph Arup. **13.3a d** W S Atkins; ph JW. **13.4a d**/ph Arup.

Chapter 14
River and canal bridges

14.1 Until the coming of the motorway, almost all road bridges were over rivers or canals. Today it is generally considered that these deserve most attention to appearance.

14.2 This chapter covers the special considerations for bridges over rivers, but comments are equally valid for bridges over docks, lakes, sea inlets and canals. Canals also have specific and separate requirements (see Paragraph 14.21 et seq.).

14.3 *It must be remembered and considered that all river and canal bridges will generally be seen by slow-moving viewers, principally on the water or along the towpath. This makes them fundamentally different from motorway overbridges, which are primarily seen at high speed from vehicles. Also, the slow-moving viewing public will generally be in a more tranquil environment. It is therefore inappropriate to*

express and emphasize the dynamism, flow and speed of the road traffic in the bridge, as one would normally do on a motorway bridge. Emphasis on vertical elements can help the expression of stability and tranquillity, as opposed to flow and dynamism. Vertical elements breaking the parapet, square or circular features in an ornamental parapet, and other vertical architectural elements, such as obelisks, ornamental lamps or statuary, either along or at the ends of bridges, can be suitable in various situations. Arched forms are particularly good at expressing stability and tranquillity, and have an appropriate traditional association with rivers.

14.4 The topography in which the river sits has the greatest influence on the design of the bridge. As one proceeds up-river it can be divided into:
• a flat plain with a river or estuary
• a broad valley with a river or multiple watercourses in the valley bottom
• a river in a deep, established channel
• a river in a gorge, where the gorge dominates.
These give rise to generic forms with particular problems.

14.1a (above) RIVER YARRA BRIDGE, Melbourne. Attention to appearance does *not* mean fussy, overblown, irrational design such as this.

14.3a (right) MARSH MILLS VIADUCT, River Plym, Devon: how *not* to cross a river. It is better to keep junctions clear of river crossings, expecially with complex topography. The dynamic motor traffic should not be dominant.

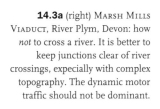

14.5 A flat plain requires approach viaducts to rise up to a major span giving a hog-curve, especially where high navigational clearances are required. The approach spans can look very dominant and unpleasant in a flat plain or estuary. Maximizing the length of embankment and the drama of the main river span can draw attention away from the approach viaducts. Trees, buildings and the topography should be used to minimize the visibility of the approaches, and they should be kept as simple as possible. Acute angles of view emphasize the approach viaducts, and this view should be considered.

14.6 A broad valley requires a viaduct to span from valley side to valley side (see Chapter 6). Embankments should be avoided, since they would tend to distort the form of the valley side and the natural visual flow of the valley. Preferably, abutments should spring from the steepest part of the valley side (see Chapter 4 and Fig. 6.36a). The span or spans crossing the main water channel should acknowledge and celebrate the river crossing. The vertical profile should be approximately level or have a slight hog-curve. Views through and under the viaduct, and in particular through the main span, are very important and should be considered both from moving viewpoints (footpaths and navigable waterways) and fixed points, both public and private. Approach embankments should not encroach on important views.

14.5a (right) Queen Elizabeth II Bridge, Dartford. Approach viaducts are very dominant.

14.5b (below) Sunshine Skyway Bridge, Tampa Bay, Florida. Single plane of cables gives clarity of form. Also note the extensive and unattractive protection against ship impact. The drama of the main span draws the eye away from the approach span.

14.6a (below) Border Bridge, Berwick-upon-Tweed: excellent views under and through the bridge.

14.6b (bottom) Severn Bridge, Bridgnorth: classic river span and approach viaducts.

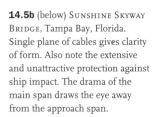

14.7b (left) CHARLES DE GAULLE BRIDGE, Paris: on axis of adjacent streets and with approaches landscaped and utilizing quai levels.

14.7a (below) GUADARAMA BRIDGE, Herrera, Spain. Bold geometry expresses the span well.

14.8a (above) SNEBRA GHYLL BRIDGE, Hensingham: dramatic gorge crossed dramatically.

14.8b (left) FOOTBRIDGE, Merthyr Tydfil, Wales: use of natural abutment.

14.7 An established river channel, as is usually the case in towns and cities, and on a smaller scale in valleys, should have the watercourse itself crossed with the main span or spans. Any approach spans should be treated in a separate but integrated way. In rural areas, embankments are often best for the approaches, to separate and emphasize the river span. In urban areas they should be part of the built environment, related in townscape terms to the adjacent built form and local character. Also, in urban areas it is best to integrate the levels and axis of the bridge with the adjacent road network.

14.8 A gorge or steep valley, where the watercourse is a relatively small though important item to cross, needs a slightly different approach. The bridge or viaduct should cross the valley from side to side visually. The abutments should be directly into the hillside or rock face, and embankments should generally be avoided, unless they can be made to look as though they are the natural topography. The setout of the piers or columns should be carefully designed to span the watercourse clearly. Dramatic sites generally call for dramatic structural solutions (see Chapter 2), and often the difficulties of erection and access encourage this. Drama should not be down-played.

14.9 Reflections of the bridge in the water and off the water on the soffit are important and need consideration.

Where a semicircular arch is used it is particularly important to have the springing line at the usual water level, to give a circle with the reflection. The effect of the bridge with its reflection in the water should be drawn in perspective and then fine-tuned to achieve a satisfactory effect. The reflection of a black or dark soffit can be particularly unpleasant. The dappled reflections of water on the underside of a bridge can be very pleasant in their own right and can also give more light under a bridge for pedestrians. Maximum light penetration under a river bridge should always be sought. This can be helped by increasing the edge cantilever to reduce the overall breadth of the longitudinal beams, by keeping the edge of the

deck as slender as possible, and by maximizing the clear height, especially at the edges of the deck. The dappled effect is best exploited with the curved planar soffit of masonry or concrete arches, and in the flat soffit of cantilevers. Light reflecting through trusses and trussed arches can be very pleasant. Leaf piers, especially where they project to the outer edge of the deck, tend to block the penetration of reflected light. The reflection of the bridge when illuminated should also be considered (see also Chapter 11, Paragraph 11.7).

14.10 Traditionally people have stood on bridges to watch the river, to fish or even to play Pooh Sticks. Whilst ensuring that there is no conflict or danger with traffic and pedestrians, there is no reason to discourage this important usage! On major new river crossings, on new bridges near historic bridges or with a view of other important sights, there may be a need or desire to allow for viewing points, i.e. the modern equivalent of refuges over cutwaters on medieval bridges, as well as designing the parapets for seeing over. Where there is particularly heavy pedestrian usage, as on bridges near commuter stations like Blackfriars (Fig. 22.9a), viewpoints can avoid conflict with traffic or pedestrian congestion.

14.10a (above) GUETIN BRIDGE, River Nievre, France: pedestrian viewing point added to exploit views.

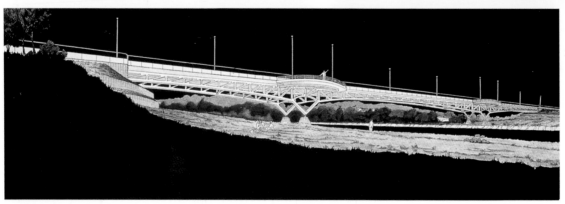

14.9a (top) ROIZE BRIDGE, France. Thin edge and trussed beam give good light penetration.

14.9b (above, centre) MOLE BRIDGE, East Molesey, Surrey. Reflected light under the bridge is important.

14.10b (above) LAVAL BRIDGE, River Mayenne, France: cantilevered viewing galleries.

14.11a (left) Bᴙɪᴅsᴛᴏᴡ Bᴙɪᴅɢᴇ, Ross-on-Wye, Hereford & Worcester: good attention to detail of stone abutment.

14.14a (below) Usᴋ Bᴙɪᴅɢᴇ, Abergavenny, Wales: boulder river entraining.

14.13a (left) Bᴙɪᴅsᴛᴏᴡ Bᴙɪᴅɢᴇ: simple stone steps up embankment.

14.13b (above) Pᴏɴᴛ ᴅᴇ ʟᴀ Tᴏᴜᴙɴᴇʟʟᴇ, Paris: pedestrian access stair incorporated in retaining wall.

14.11 Since river and canal bridges are seen by slow-moving pedestrians and boat users, the quantity and quality of detail are very important. Surface texture and modelling are necessary (see Chapters 5 and 23). Natural materials such as stone, brick and timber are particularly appropriate for river and canal bridges.

14.12 Where there are multiple spans, those crossing the navigable channel and opening spans should express their particular function (see Chapter 15). Navigable spans are often higher or longer and may need navigation lights. These should be expressed but must form part of an integrated total structure. Such differences should not be artificially concealed. The masts or towers of cable-stay structures, suspension bridges and overhead balance lifting bridges can be exploited to express the special functions.

14.13 Pedestrian access onto the bridge deck from the riverbank is often necessary and should not be an afterthought. In urban areas this can be used to integrate the abutments into the townscape (see Chapter 16) by making them more architectural. In rural areas, steps and ramps should be integrated into the embankments in liaison with the landscape architect. Steps in rural areas are best in natural rustic materials, such as stone or timber. They are also best in a zig-zag or diagonal to the slope, rather than straight up it. Steps can be particularly obtrusive, especially when in precast concrete, if not designed carefully.

14.14 Unnatural entraining of the river banks, and moving the course of a natural river, should be avoided wherever possible. The appearance of the river should be as natural as possible in rural areas (this also gives access for wildlife). Close co-operation between the bridge designer

14.14b (right) Landquart Bridge, Serneus, Switzerland: excellent use of boulders for river entraining.

14.14c (below) Brocking Footbridge, Surrey: a simple treatment, well modelled, and of the correct scale.

14.14d (above) Mole Bridge, East Molesey, Surrey. The setting of the Lutyens bridge is ruined by insensitive river entraining.

14.15a (right) M18 Thorne Viaduct, South Yorkshire: delicate columns positioned clear of navigable channel and floodwater.

(engineer and/or architect) and the landscape architect is vital. (See Chapter 27 for more information on natural treatment under bridges.) In urban areas where the river is already entrained, an appearance related to the adjacent entraining walls should be produced. Utilitarian finishes such as sheet piling or in situ concrete can be suitable where a similar treatment to the river wall is adjacent, but would be inappropriate where adjacent walls are brick or stone or have an architectural treatment. In such cases the treatment should be either identical to the existing, where it forms a small part of a larger river wall, or could be a reinterpretation in the same idiom of an existing, more architectural treatment, where the length of river wall affected is significant. Where the treatment is architectural, it should be designed by an architect.

14.15 Piers on land can often be more slender than on road overbridges, since there are usually no vehicle impact load requirements. This can be exploited for a more light and elegant bridge.

14.16 Piers in non-navigable rivers and flood plains need to contend with impact from flotsam, and should be designed not to catch or retain it or to cause unnecessary turbulence, which might also create scour. Rounded and/or pointed cutwaters, leaf piers or columns are thus generally necessary and should be exploited for their inherent character and beauty. Where rivers are prone to flooding, the cutwater is traditionally curved convexly inwards above the normal water level in an inverted boat shape. This can give extra flood capacity and avoids boats or flotsam coming to rest on a flat-topped cutwater. This can be particularly characterful and interesting. It can be further exploited to deter vandalism on low river bridges where haunched or variable depth steel or concrete beams can sit on such an inverted, boat-shaped pier, rather than on stumpy columns.

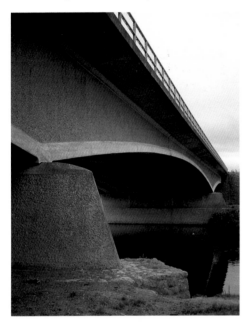

14.16a (far left) BRIDSTOW BRIDGE M50, Ross-on-Wye: elegant modelled cutwaters.

14.16b (left) M3 THAMES BRIDGE, Chertsey: elegant, sharp-arrised cutwaters.

14.16c (below) TAW BRIDGE, Devon: poor proportions of leaf piers.

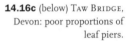

14.16d (above) PERTH BRIDGE, Scotland. Short piers make the variable depth spans dominant.

14.16e (right) PONT ROYAL, Paris. Overlap of short pier and variable depth haunch gives elegant effect.

14.18a (left) TORRIDGE BRIDGE, Devon: out-of-scale ship impact piers.

14.17 The rounded or pointed cutwaters on masonry arched bridges can be extended up to form pedestrian reserves or embrasures (see Paragraph 14.10 above). This can help to give a more vertical emphasis to the bridge, and can be useful where extra mass is needed to stabilize masonry arches (see Chapter 3). On masonry faced arches the same treatment can improve the bridge modelling, avoiding the 'wallpaper' effect of applied masonry cladding. Such cutwaters/embrasures are visually better in loadbearing masonry, which may be possible where no vehicle loads are required.

14.18 Ship impact can be a major determinant of bridge design on navigable rivers, particularly in estuaries, where ships are bigger and heavier. Unless all superstructure of the bridge is kept beyond the navigable envelope (this is especially critical on arched forms beneath the deck), large islands or ship impact posts will be required, extending well above high tide or flood level. These are invariably hideous, like Wellington boots on a ballerina.

The islands or posts are best avoided by careful design, or minimized in size, height and number. Islands for adjacent structures should not be joined together. The utilization of natural river islands for bridge piers is visually highly desirable. Piers near the edge of the river are better on the bank to avoid the need for ship impact islands. On ship canals, where the prow or side of the ship may overhang the bank, additional clearance may be necessary to avoid the need for

14.18b (below) A48 NEWPORT BRIDGE, South Wales: massive piers in tidal river.

protection. Where span limitations or other factors prevent piers near the bank from being actually on it, sometimes the bank can be artificially extended out to form ship protection. This is preferable generally to a ship protection island or bollards; however, the extended river bank should be designed by the landscape architect to appear natural. Where no ship impact protection is required, e.g. in shallow water, visually it can be excellent for the pier to stand in the water.

Where ship impact islands are unavoidable, provision of appropriate landscaping and encouragement of wildlife are desirable, using natural materials such as broken rock. The outward-leaning shape of ships' hulls can dictate the shape of the top of ship impact islands, and this can be exploited to give interesting sculptural shapes for the top section of the island.

When designing river bridges, the ship impact islands or posts should always be drawn or preferably modelled at both high and low water where appropriate, so that the true appearance of the bridge can be judged in all water conditions.

Navigation lights and warning signs are often required on ship impact islands, and these should be considered at the early stages of design, not as an afterthought.

14.19 The soffit on river bridges is visually more important than on road overbridges, as it is seen by slow-moving pedestrians and boat users (see Paragraph 14.3 above) as they pass underneath. This means that more care should be taken over the appearance of the soffit to make it tidy, well co-ordinated, elegantly detailed and modelled, and with visual interest derived from the structure, form and materials. Decoration is generally not appropriate. Services carried on the bridge, such as water mains, gas pipes, power cables, etc., should be co-ordinated and concealed, especially where they pass from the abutment onto the deck soffit. Forms of structure which give visual interest on the soffit should be chosen, e.g. arched structures, concrete box beams with wide cantilevers, cantilevers supported on brackets, composite construction with minimal longitudinal beams, and maximum cross-cantilever members.

14.20 Footbridges over water do not need to comply with technical requirements for road bridges, and therefore have much more freedom of design. This should be exploited (see Chapter 12). Materials and form should respond to the setting, and can be an enjoyable and significant part of a pedestrian route (Fig. 2.20a). Anything from the most sophisticated technology to simple stepping stones can be appropriate.

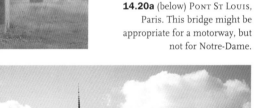

14.19a (far left) Touche Bridge, Toulouse: structure designed to give visual interest to soffit.

14.19b (left) A27 Adur Bridge, Shoreham-by-Sea, West Sussex. Cantilever brackets give visual interest.

14.20a (below) Pont St Louis, Paris. This bridge might be appropriate for a motorway, but not for Notre-Dame.

14.19c (above) Adhamiyah Bridge, Iraq: elegant soffit design.

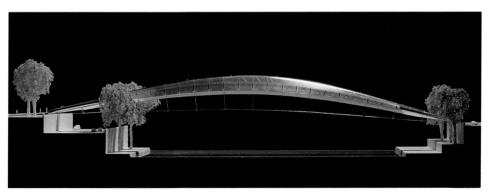

14.20b (right) Solferino Footbridge, Paris: exploits design freedom.

14.21a (below) A5 Freeth
Bridge: traditional rural bridge.

14.21b (below) Measham Bridge,
Ashby Canal, Leicester: traditional
urban bridge, now demolished.

14.21e (above) Gargrave
Lock Bridge, North Yorkshire.
Canals have individual character
which should be retained.

14.21c (centre, left) Coventry
Canal Bridge, Leicestershire:
traditional stone bridge.

14.21d (left) Herengracht Canal
Bridge, Amsterdam: the quality of
detail to be aspired to.

14.21 *Canals have particular requirements in addition to or different from river bridges*, principally due to their historic and man-made nature. Canals were designed and built over great lengths as single entities, and maintained as such. This means that each has its individual character, with a suite of bridges, street furniture, signs and towpath details, similar for the entire length, though with variations to accommodate the use of local materials.

14.22 As with river bridges, canal bridges are viewed at a slow pace and close up, but since canals are now principally for leisure usage, *the continuity of visual experience as boat users pass slowly along a canal to appreciate the landscape and heritage of the inland waterway system is of primary importance in the appearance of the bridge.*

14.23 Increasingly, many canals are conservation areas for considerable parts of their length, and the need to build in sympathy with and preferably to enhance a conservation area can be taken as a useful starting point for all bridges in the canal environment. This does *not* mean, however, that a pastiche of historic bridges is called for; this would be inappropriate for modern usage, road widths and vertical profile. False arched façades in front of simple beam bridges are to be particularly discouraged, not only for appearance reasons, but also to avoid danger to boaters emerging from dark tunnels and not perceiving the true soffit position.

14.24 *There are two preferred options:*

● *a thoroughly modern, dramatic design, well thought out for its specific location*
● *a low-key design responding to the historic forms, materials, proportions and details of the canal environment.*

14.25 Historically, the forms of canal bridges derived from local materials and their appropriate methods of construction, which can be still as valid today. Also, they derived from functions such as the need to prevent towropes from snagging and the requirement to keep horses pulling the barges without having to stop and start, or even the need for bargees to walk their boats by foot along tunnel soffits. These are no longer valid for new bridges.

14.26 Canal bridges traditionally were not a kit of parts; the appearance and proportion of the whole bridge were always considered and still should be. Canal bridges should be

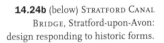

14.24a (left) Bathurst Basin Swing Bridge, Bristol: modern, dramatic design.

14.24b (below) Stratford Canal Bridge, Stratford-upon-Avon: design responding to historic forms.

14.26a (below) M1 Northampton Arm Canal Bridge. Unusual bridge, but the vehicles are too obtrusive.

14.26b (below, right) Rochdale Canal Bridge, Oldham. Decorative metal balustrade terminated by pilasters helps express stable form.

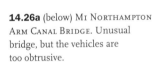

stable objects in the landscape, and the horizontal flow of the vehicles should not be emphasized. Since the spans are generally small, brick or stone pilasters can logically be used to break horizontal elements, and to terminate parapets or turn corners. Canal bridges are best designed to terminate at a visual stop, not to flow into the landscape beyond. Simple and appropriately robust ornamental elements can be used in metal balustrades to break the horizontal flow. All these elements should be used to define the proportions.

14.27 *The two basic forms of canal bridge – still valid today – are the simple single arch and the masonry 'book end' with simple span beam.* The masonry 'book end' should have a masonry parapet, and the simple beam should have a different form of parapet, often metal. This helps the static feeling of the bridge and helps define the elements. The masonry arch form should have a masonry parapet which flows into preferably curving masonry wingwalls.

14.28 Canal bridges were traditionally curving in plan and elevation, which is a structurally logical way to use masonry in a retaining wall. The curving top of the parapet was intended originally to ease the passage of towropes, which is now rarely relevant, but can give a very beautiful

and appropriate form that should be exploited. Battered walls, where used locally, are also a logical solution to a masonry retaining or loadbearing wall, and can be used.

14.29 The span over the canal and its towpath is best kept single, without side spans. The use of side spans for pedestrians and main span for the watercourse, which is very appropriate to rivers, is inappropriate to canals.

14.30 The exception to Paragraph 14.29 is when the structure is spanning more than just the canal and at some considerable height, i.e. when a viaduct crosses a valley, and the canal is just one element in the valley to be crossed (see Paragraph 14.8 above). The parapet need not then be solid for the canal users and probably should be open for vehicle passengers to appreciate the view.

14.31 The parapet is best solid and in masonry where a road passes over the canal. An open parapet draws the attention to fast-moving vehicles, especially where traffic is close to the parapet due to no pedestrian usage. A solid parapet also helps prevent vehicle lights dazzling boat users and affecting their night vision, and avoids the possibility of unsightly later additions of light screening.

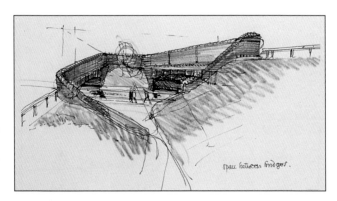

14.28a (below) BLACK COUNTRY SPINE ROAD: curved brickwork enhances the canal environment.

14.26c (above, left) A4091 FAZELEY BRIDGE, Staffordshire: modern concrete portal frame bridge with pilasters and string-course, spoilt by awkward skew.

14.27a (left) GLOUCESTER AND SHARPNESS CANAL BRIDGE, Gloucester: 'book end' type bridge.

14.32a (left) Bingley Locks, West Yorkshire: stone and timber in new canal structure under construction.

14.32b (below) A650 Bingley Bypass, West Yorkshire: new stone retaining wall adjacent to canal.

14.32c (left) Minshull Street Bridge, Rochdale Canal, Manchester: traditional brick walls with rounded copings.

14.33a (above) Gargrave Bridge, North Yorkshire: 1930s concrete canal bridge with appropriate modelling.

14.32 The extensive use of masonry walls, in brick or stone depending on the locality, is traditional to the canal environment, and is to be encouraged.

14.33 Concrete bridges were common over canals in the early 20th century and are still appropriate. Because of their short spans and solid parapets, they will inevitably appear heavy and massive. In the canal context, light, slender and elegant concrete bridges can be difficult to achieve and inappropriate. An emphasis on geometry and faceting or modelling of the surface is appropriate. The use of curving wingwalls in both plan and elevation is appropriate to concrete (though double curvature should be avoided) and has an affinity with canal forms.

14.34 *Colour schemes and details, such as signs for bridge numbers, should match those on the rest of the canal.* Traditional colour schemes are usually black and white.

Towpaths should usually be reinstated to incorporate operational canal features such as stop plank grooves and approach fenders.

PICTURE CREDITS
14.1a ph Muriel Bankhead. **14.3a** ph JW. **14.5a d** Dartford River Crossing Ltd; ph Robjohn. **14.5b d** Fritz Leonhardt/Figg and Muller Engineers Inc.; ph Jean Muller. **14.6a d** Lowry and Woodhouse. **14.6b d** Gifford. **14.7a d** Carlos Millán y Francisco Iniesta. **14.7b d** Karesinski. **14.8a d** Allott and Lomax. **14.8b** ph JW. **14.9a d** Jean Muller. **14.9b d** Edwin Lutyens; ph JW. **14.10a d** Alain Spielmann. **14.10b d** Alain Spielmann. **14.11a** ph JW. **14.13a** ph JW. **14.13b** ph JW. **14.14a** ph JW. **14.14b** ph JW. **14.14c** ph JW. **14.14d d** Edwin Lutyens; ph JW. **14.15a** ph JW. **14.16a d** Scott Wilson Kirkpatrick; ph JW. **14.16b** ph JW. **14.16c d** Rust; ph JW. **14.16d** ph JW. **14.16e** ph JW. **14.18a d** Rust; ph JW. **14.19a d** Alain Spielmann; ph JW. **14.19b** ph JW. **14.19c d** Yee Associates/Maunsell; ph A Wallace. **14.20a** ph JW. **14.20b d** Future Systems. **14.21d** ph JW. **14.21e** ph JW. **14.24a** ph JW. **14.24b** ph JW. **14.26a d** Owen Williams. **14.26b d**/ph Arup. **14.27a** ph JW. **14.28a d** Percy Thomas Partnership; illus Ron Weeks. **14.32a** ph JW. **14.32b** ph JW. **14.32c** ph JW. **14.33a** ph JW.

Chapter 15

Opening bridges

15.1 The various types of movable bridges – swing, bascule, vertical lift, transporter, etc. – all present special problems, particularly rolling lift bridges with their high curved ends. It would be impracticable to generalize about movable bridges, other than to stress that their natures and the prominent positions they often occupy call for special care to achieve satisfactory solutions, appropriate to their settings, in both open and closed positions.

15.2 *Their unusual form and the fact that they move will inevitably attract attention, so it is best to emphasize both form and mechanism through bold use of structure and colour.*

15.2a (below) SHAD THAMES FOOTBRIDGE, London: celebration of the mechanism.

15.2b (right) ST KATHARINE DOCK, London: elegant steel lifting bridge.

15.2c (bottom) ST KATHARINE'S DOCK: traditional but well-proportioned timber lifting bridge.

15.2d (right) Cross Keys Swing Bridge, Lincolnshire: road/rail bridge converted to two-lane road bridge.

15.2e (below) Kingsferry Bridge, Isle of Sheppey, Kent: bold, though visually heavy form.

15.2f (left) Marken, Holland: traditional bold expression of mechanism for canal lift bridge.

15.5a (left) St Katharine's Dock: award-winning control building in a conservation area.

15.3 When designing such a bridge, careful consideration should be given to the integrated design of the special street furniture, such as lifting barriers, special signs, lighting, sirens, traffic signals, etc., which can proliferate and mar the design.

15.4 Consideration should be given to suitable safe spaces for pedestrians to view the opening of the bridge, where they do not interfere with traffic, either pedestrian or vehicular.

15.5b (right) Canary Wharf Lift Bridge, London. Control building which expresses its functions well.

15.6a (below) Médoc Bridge, Bordeaux. The dramatic form of this design celebrates its opening nature and avoids approach ramps.

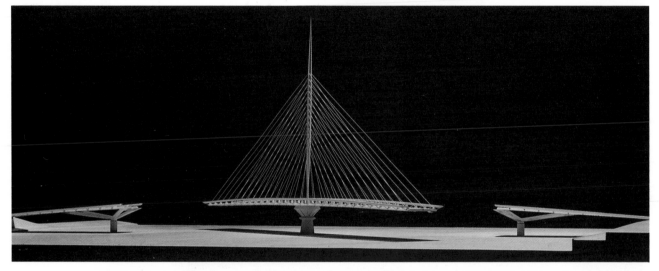

15.6c (right) Shaldon Bridge, Teignmouth, Devon. Low-key structure in a sensitive area, but the opening span is lost.

15.6b (below) Médoc Bridge, Bordeaux: elegant, unusual swing bridge design.

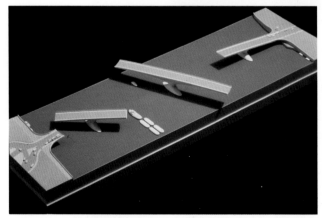

15.5 Where a control cabin is required, this can be visually prominent and can relate to the appearance of the bridge, unlike the approach normally to be taken with ancillary buildings (see Chapter 28).

15.6 Where estuarial crossings require bridges with very high clearances and thus very dominant approach viaducts, and yet the usage of the river by large vessels is very infrequent, opening bridges may be a good solution aesthetically, since the dominance of such large structures is then reduced.

Picture Credits
15.2a d/ph Whitby and Bird. **15.2b d** Arup; ph JW. **15.2c** ph JW. **15.2d d** Mott McDonald; ph JW. **15.2e** ph JW. **15.2f** ph JW. **15.5a** ph JW. **15.5b d** Alsop and Störmer; ph JW. **15.6a d** Santiago Calatrava. **15.6b d** Norman Foster. **15.6c** ph JW.

Chapter 16
Pedestrian underpasses

16.1 *Pedestrian underpasses are disliked by the public. They are seen as dark, damp, dangerous, dirty, smelly, uninviting and unpleasant.* Many people prefer to cross a busy road rather than use an underpass, which is dangerous to both pedestrian and road user. Attempting to prevent such crossing by barriers is ineffective and often more dangerous in that it stops pedestrians leaving the carriageway once they are on it.

16.2 A solution to the problem is to avoid underpasses by using controlled pedestrian crossings or pedestrian overbridges, but in some situations the geometry and levels dictate an underpass. Often they can require fewer steps or ramps to access them and the obtrusiveness of ramps to overbridges can be avoided (see Chapter 12).

16.3 *The public's (rightly or wrongly) perceived problems with underpasses* (see Paragraph 16.1) *are the problems to be resolved in the design.*

DARKNESS

16.4 The darkness can be resolved by high levels of vandal-resistant and well-maintained artificial lighting. Entrances should be broad and high and the tunnel length as short as possible to maximize natural lighting. Finishes, especially to floors, should be light in colour and have a high reflectance to maximize daylight penetration and enhance artificial light. Faceting or texturing of walls should be angled to minimize the darker-shaded facets.

DAMPNESS

16.5 Dampness can be resolved by draining the underpass, preferably with natural falls. The drainage must be easily maintainable. Where animals use the underpass, especially cattle, a raised pedestrian walkway drained to fall to the lower level can help avoid pedestrians having to negotiate mud, dung and floodwater when the drains get blocked. Dampness from dripping walls should be avoided by adequate damp-proofing. Keeping a clear path for the wind to blow through by avoiding retaining walls opposite entrances helps clear damp and smells (see Paragraph 16.6 for other advantages).

DANGER

16.6 To reduce perceived danger, the view in and out must not be blocked by bends, nor by walls or planting facing the entrance to the underpass. There should be no flank walls at right angles to the entrance to form a place for attackers to hide. Maximizing the width of the underpass gives space to walk past well clear of other users. The inclusion of a cycle way or equestrian path can give this extra width, but there should

16.6a (left) COVENTRY GREYFRIARS. The park flows through the underpass.

16.1a (above) TOWER OF LONDON: narrow, dark, unpleasant underpass with vagrants.

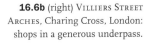

16.6b (right) VILLIERS STREET ARCHES, Charing Cross, London: shops in a generous underpass.

be no railing separating the users, since this defeats the purpose. A kerb and possibly a change of surface or a row of bollards are all that may be needed. Ramping the floor surface up to meet the wall and ceiling gives extra width for a psychological escape zone, as well as other advantages (see Paragraph 16.7). Where the approach ramp is in cutting, this slope should continue as the ramped paving internally, either on the same plane or angled or swept at the entrances. In urban areas with underpass complexes, incorporating shops to increase activity helps overcome perceived danger.

DIRT

16.7 Underpasses are seen as dirty partly due to maintenance and flooding (see Paragraph 16.5), but largely because of graffiti. The treatment of the walls using murals can improve the appearance and reduce graffiti, especially on existing structures (see Chapter 23), but avoidance of walls is the best option, since floors and ceilings are rarely popular for graffiti for practical reasons. The ceiling can be arched or sloped down to meet the wall at

approximately the position that the sloped floor (see Paragraph 16.6 above) rises to meet it, giving an approximately lens-shaped cross-section. Alternatively, the ramped floor can meet the ceiling. The use of sacrificial wax-based, hot-water-soluble graffiti coatings can be of advantage, but other coatings appear to have little benefit in that they either have an unpleasant appearance themselves or leave a residue in crevices after cleaning. Frequent repainting over existing graffiti is often a practical solution on existing structures but gives a long-term maintenance problem.

SMELL

16.8 Underpasses are often smelly for two reasons. Firstly the configuration can prevent through drafts, which remove damp smells (see Paragraph 16.5); secondly they get used as toilets. This tends to happen when there are places with suitable walls that cannot be seen, so the provision against perceived danger in Paragraph 16.6, giving through visibility, no hiding places and no walls, will also avoid the problem of smells.

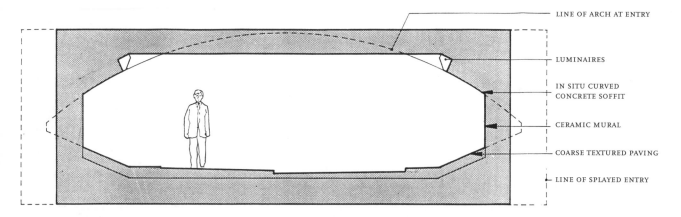

LINE OF ARCH AT ENTRY

LUMINAIRES

IN SITU CURVED CONCRETE SOFFIT

CERAMIC MURAL

COARSE TEXTURED PAVING

LINE OF SPLAYED ENTRY

CROSS SECTION 1:50

16.7a (above) BOUNDS GREEN UNDERPASS, London: the best shape for an underpass in cutting. Note the increased height and width at the entrance.

16.7b (left) WESTERN BANK BRIDGE, Sheffield University: walls avoided entirely.

16.9a (far left) Old Street
Underpass, London. Entrance
feature draws attention
to entrance.

16.9b (left) Paris Métro
Entrance: distinctive and inviting.

Uninviting Appearance

16.9 The uninviting nature of underpasses is due to the appearance of the entrance and its approaches, the relationship of the underpass to desire lines, and the visibility of the entrance locations. The entrance should be large, well-lit and attractive. Enlarging the entrance makes it seem more generous and welcoming and gives the optical trick of making the tunnel appear shorter when you are in it. The entrance should be at the natural flow of the landscape, ground modelling, and pedestrian routes. The line of the route should appear to follow desire lines, since having ramps running away from where you wish to go discourages the use of the underpass. Ideally the flow of the landscape should indicate the entrance and exit without the need for signs, but this is rarely practical. Entrance and exit features both visible from the approach always help orientation, and are vital to announce the presence of the underpass and its destination in urban areas. Being able to see the exit from the entrance is always more inviting than entering a dark hole in the ground. Where there is a network of underground passages, a map at each entrance is important. In principle, such troglodyte complexes for pedestrians should be avoided.

Pleasant Places

16.10 Pedestrian underpasses should be pleasant places. The form of the space, and the quantity and quality of detail, can be even more important than with a bridge.

16.10a (above) Ploschad Revolutsii Station, Moscow. Underpasses can learn from the quality of space and detail in metro systems.

16.9c (top) London Bridge Underpass: how *not* to make a welcoming access for pedestrians.

Much can be learnt from successful metro tunnels, especially for urban situations, and the particular skills of architects should be exploited for underpasses in such situations.

Picture Credits
16.1a ph JW. **16.6a** ph JW. **16.6b d** Terry Farrell; ph JW. **16.7a d** Design Research Unit. **16.7b d** Arup. **16.9a d** Patrick Davies; ph JW. **16.9b d** Hector Guimard; ph JW. **16.9c** ph JW. **16.10a d** Alexei Dushkin.

Chapter 17
Tunnels and underpasses

17.1 A tunnel entrance can be sharp and dramatic as one enters a hillside or a mountain, or it may be very similar to an underpass as one drives down between long retaining walls. It may be circular or parabolic if the tunnel has been bored, or rectangular if other methods of construction have been used.

17.2 The treatment of tunnel portals can be bold and impressive, with control buildings or other structures positioned over the entrance. This is usually more acceptable in an urban or semi-urban situation. In a rural setting, it may be preferable to minimize the entrance by reducing the visible structure and using more planting and natural contours in the landscape.

17.1a (below) Mont Blanc Tunnel, France: dramatic entrance.

17.1c (below, centre) Tunnel, Belgium: visually imposing portal.

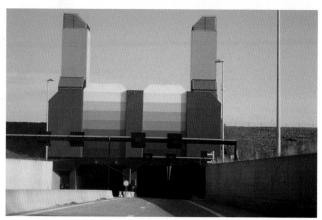

17.2b (above) Penmaenbach Tunnel, North Wales: minimum visual impact of tunnel entrance.

17.1b (above, left) Tunnel, Nice, France. Use of planters softens entrance to urban tunnel.

17.2a (left) Limehouse Link, London: massive urban structure, unattractive to some people, though suitable for its context.

17.3a (left) Hanging Lakes Tunnel, USA: extended tunnels with attractive shaping of ends.

17.4a (below) Tunnel Entrance, Aoste Vally, Italy: uninspiring plain concrete finish.

17.3 The entrance into a cliff tunnel will face the driver, and it is appropriate that the visible structure should be minimal and the effect given of a cut-off tube. The entrances on the A55 in North Wales show the required simplicity of detail. Hanging Lakes Tunnel entrances show the same principle but with attractive skewing and shaping of the tubes; being extended from the cliff face, they also give protection from falling rocks.

17.4 Headwalls across the face of the tunnel entrance are often used to retain the hillside behind, but without sensitive treatment they can appear plain and depressing. Walls should not be left with a plain finish but use made of texture or colour to enhance the visual interest. Architectural detail such as the Mont Blanc entrance (see Fig. 17.1a) can be very dramatic, while Fig. 17.4b shows an unusual use of colour, which correctly focuses the driver on the entrance.

17.5 Tunnels may run out directly onto bridge structures (see Fig. 7.21b). In these situations the structural lines and material finishes should be sympathetic. Cut-off tube tunnel entrances give better flow of lines than the headwalls across the entrance.

17.4b (above, left) Tunnel Entrance, Belgium: dramatic treatment.

17.4c (above, centre) Cuilfail Tunnel, Lewes, East Sussex. Interest is provided at entrance by sculpture.

17.5a (above) Roundhill Viaducts and Tunnels, Kent: simple tunnel entrances formed in the plane of the hillside (planting not yet fully reinstated).

17.6 In the urban environment there is usually more visible structure, hard landscaping and street furniture to arrange and co-ordinate. Again, texture and colour can be used to lighten and uplift the finish. Fig. 17.1b also shows the use of planters to soften the visual impact, and the finishes help to integrate the structure into its urban environment.

17.7 Long retaining walls will be required for underpasses and entrances to deep tunnels. Concrete finishes or cladding can be interesting and potentially colourful in an urban setting. However, if cladding is used on a tunnel approach it should co-ordinate with finishes inside the tunnel (see Chapter 29 for treatment of walls).

17.8 Immersed tube tunnels will require long entrance ramps, and these can be used for casting tunnel segments in the construction process. This can reduce environmental impact on the surrounding area by avoiding the need for a separate casting yard or dry dock; in a flat landscape, though, high walls may be needed around the entrance ramps to prevent flooding. The visual impact on the outside of these can be minimized by soft landscaping and earth mounding to reduce the visible height.

17.9 At a tunnel entrance there is a transition from outside natural daylight to artificial light. This can be controlled by changing the level of artificial light from strong near the tunnel portal to a lower level deeper into the tunnel at a

17.7a (above) Abbey Foregate, Shrewsbury: attractive brickwork to walls but fussy detail on parapet.

17.7b (right) Holloway Tunnel, Birmingham: strong use of colour.

position by which the eyes will have adjusted. Where the tunnel has approach ramps, the transition can also be assisted by the use of darker wall finishes near the tunnel entrance and by overhead louvres near the entrance to provide shade.

17.10 Twin tunnels will usually be required for dual carriageways. Depending upon the form of construction, they may be separated by a thin wall or by several metres of rock. The treatment of entrances and of the splitter wall may be governed by this separation: if the separation is small the portal entrance will be one structure, but if the separation is great they may be treated individually. When the carriageways are immediately adjacent, the splitter wall should appear appropriately robust to carry its load but not unnaturally wide. When carriageways are separated, as with twin bores, they should be sufficiently wide apart to allow each bore to appear visually strong in its own right.

17.11 Landtake requirements will vary for different types of construction. Extensive landscape treatment will be required for cut-and-cover construction but minimized by bored tunnels. In rural areas the original landscape is generally reinstated over cut-and-cover, but in urban areas there may be soft landscape, hard landscape, buildings or all three in the townscape design. In all cases this should be carefully designed, and sufficient depth of cover and loading capacity should be allowed. The requirements for construction of segments or disposal of spoil may require considerable landtake around tunnel entrances, with consequences for landscaping on completion. Restrictions on land in urban areas may suggest that tunnels for two-way flow should be constructed one above another. All aspects of construction and their consequences must be considered in the design process.

17.12 Light-coloured finishes on the walls and ceiling of tunnels will enhance visibility. In two-lane tunnels a dark ceiling can be considered, as drivers may relate to the side walls, which may reflect sufficient light. The dark ceiling might be preferred to reduce requirements for washing, but it could be visually oppressive. In wider tunnels a light ceiling is preferred, to improve reflectivity and to give a back-drop to silhouette vehicles ahead.

17.12a (below)
FREDERIKSSUNDSUEY TUNNEL,
Denmark: attractive dark ceiling
with light walls.

17.13 Finishes within a tunnel must withstand a harsh environment and be durable against fire, water and automotive pollution. They should not be high gloss as this may cause glare in reflections off the walls and should also have good sound absorption qualities.

PICTURE CREDITS
17.1a ph JW. **17.1b** ph Arup. **17.1c** ph Eternit. **17.2a d** Sir Alexander Gibb & Partners; ph AMEC. **17.2b d** Travers Morgan. **17.3a d** Gruen Associates. **17.4a** ph Alliance Ceramics, Steel Products. **17.4b** ph JW. **17.5a d** Mott Macdonald; ph Tony Gee. **17.7a d**/ph Gifford & Partners. **17.7b d** Birmingham City Council; ph Alliance Ceramics, Steel Products. **17.12a** ph Alliance Ceramics, Steel Products.

Chapter 18

Culverts

18.1 *When culverts are rectangular and of similar sizes to bridges, they should be treated as bridges or as accommodation underpasses*, with wingwalls in line with the channel to minimize their visibility.

18.2 *When culverts are circular or elliptical*, whether in situ concrete, precast pipe or corrugated steel tube, *they should be treated similarly to tunnel portals*, i.e. cut off parallel to the embankment slope through which they penetrate, and with a slender, simple concrete edge.

18.3 Headwalls should be avoided unless they can be incorporated with retaining walls or other parts of structures.

18.4 Where an upstand is required at the portal to prevent soil slippage over the culvert, it is better to slope this wall back approximately 45°, so that the wall appears as a bell mouth or sloping soffit and a slender edge is emphasized. With circular or elliptical culverts, the bell mouth continued at the sides can help in avoiding turbulence and blockage at the entrance in times of flood by guiding debris through.

18.5 Where a series of culverts is close together, it is better to combine them visually to give a portal of repeated arches or a linear trabeated structure. With circular and elliptical culverts, it is generally better to have a series of smaller openings rather than a single large one, if that would mean a higher crown and thus a more obtrusive structure.

18.6 Where culverts can be combined with pedestrian underpasses, this should generally be done, since it increases the space in the pedestrian underpass and can deter graffiti. The combined structure should then be treated as a pedestrian underpass (see Chapter 16).

18.7 On new culverts, fencing to indicate the presence of a steep drop over 1.5m is required, placed on or preferably just behind the coping or portal edge. There should be insufficient space between the edge and the fence for access, or for maintenance staff to need to enter to maintain landscaping. The barrier should be as unobtrusive as possible, and should not be visually more dominant than the culvert to which it is ancillary.

18.8 Extended concrete headwalls, plain aluminium or galvanized steel railings, especially modular panels with crude, cumbersome joints and heavy timber post and rail fencing are not recommended. Tensioned wire on slender, black light metal posts set in the landscaping just behind the

18.5a (above) A332, WINDSOR: excellent cut-off culverts.

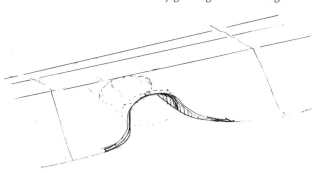

18.4a (top) CULVERT MOUTH: bell mouth cut-off culvert.

18.5b (above) A15 MOXEY SOUTH DRAIN: an unusual combination of culverts in a simple, elegant, rustic stone headwall.

18.7a (left) CULVERT ON A303, Andover, Hampshire: an elegant example, kept below 1.5m to avoid the need for ugly barriers.

18.7b (far left) A3 WISLEY, Surrey: simple railing, but too urban and preferable in dark brown or green.

18.7c (left) A17, HUNDRED DRAIN BRIDGE: simple traditional protection.

18.10a (left) CONCRETE CULVERT ENTRANCE, Gloucester: to be avoided.

18.9a (above) CULVERT WITH STONE PITCHING, Ross-on-Wye.

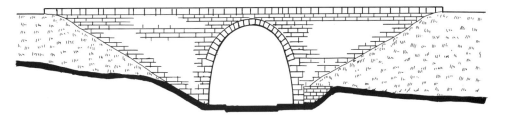

18.12a (right) STONE HEADWALL, Germany: elegantly detailed.

portal edge is generally the preference, since this tends to disappear into the landscaping from a distance. Circular timber posts with tensioned wire can also be acceptable. Where the extra strength of a metal guardrail is required, it is often best painted dark green, dark brown or black to be unobtrusive.

18.9 Hard paving on the embankment surface around the culvert portal is rarely necessary and is generally unsightly. Stone pitching is preferable, using local stone.

18.10 When a small stream in a ditch passes through an embankment, protection to the banks is often required beyond the culvert. Gabions or large rocks are generally best, so that the stream appears as natural as possible. Concrete linings and retaining walls, and steel sheet piling, should be positively discouraged.

18.11 Where a culvert penetrates a retaining wall, it should be expressed in keeping with the retaining wall, and the opportunity taken to use it as a design feature to add visual interest to the retaining wall (see Figs. 5.8a and 5.14a).

18.12 When a short embankment crosses a small hollow or ditch it can be appropriate, when consistent with the landscaping concept, to form a headwall up to the road level and face it with stone or brick. This is then effectively a small bridge. The parapet should be consistent with the concept (see Fig. 5.5d).

PICTURE CREDITS
18.5a ph JW. **18.7a d** Hampshire County Council. **18.7b** ph JW. **18.9a** ph JW. **18.10a** ph JW. **18.12a d** Leonhardt.

Chapter 19

Bridges over widened motorways

19.1 Widening of roads, especially motorways, affects the majority of existing bridges. This chapter is mainly concerned with the effect of road widening on overbridges. Underbridge widening is considered in Chapter 26.

19.2 Motorways are the most difficult and demanding roads to widen as traffic must be kept flowing with minimal restriction. The use of alternative routes is usually prohibited due to traffic volumes and congestion. The replacement or modification of existing overbridges will have a major effect on traffic. Speed of construction and safety are additional considerations and will have a major influence on the form of structure. Hence the appearance of the bridge is strongly influenced by construction restraints.

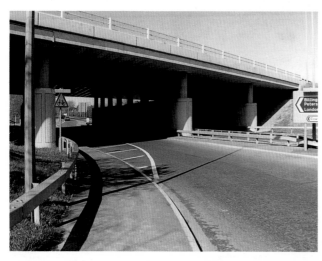

19.4a (above) A23: clumsy strengthening to piers on trunk road bridge supporting motorway.

19.3 Motorways can be widened using a range of techniques, which will have different consequences for the existing overbridges. The methods include:
● rapid widening within the existing fence lines
● symmetric – new lanes each side of the existing motorway
● asymmetric – new construction extending the motorway to one side
● parallel – a new carriageway built alongside the existing motorway and the existing two carriageways combined.

The choice of method and layout depends on the level of traffic, physical or geographical constraints, layout of existing bridges (over and under) and construction sequence.

19.4 In most cases the existing overbridges will have insufficient span or clearance to accommodate the new carriageway layout. However, a key feature of rapid widening schemes is retention of the bridges, as they can govern the speed and cost of construction. In this instance the widened carriageways are aligned through the existing spans by slightly reducing lane or hard shoulder widths. Intermediate support piers may need to be strengthened, and the treatment to the piers and the provision of additional protection using safety fences or barriers need to be handled carefully so that the character of the bridge is not unduly affected.

19.5 For other types of widening schemes, total replacement of the overbridges is needed in order to satisfy the new carriageway layout, due to obstruction by existing piers or abutments. Traffic levels on motorways at peak times usually prevent the imposition of lane restrictions. The construction of intermediate supports within existing or new central reserves may not be possible, due to inadequate working space, safety considerations or unacceptable traffic disruption. Consequently, new overbridges for symmetric and asymmetric widening schemes will need to have long single spans that

19.4b (right) M25 MOTORWAY: rapid widening through existing bridges, requiring additional retaining walls for slope stabilization. Geo textiles and gabions can also be used.

19.5a (below) M40 MOTORWAY:
wingwalls parallel to motorway.

19.5b (above) M5 MOTORWAY:
wingwalls parallel to side road.

19.6a (left) M5 MOTORWAY:
asymmetric bridge over parallel
widened motorway – visually
unbalanced.

19.6b (below) Model of
proposed bridge for parallel
widened motorway with
effective use of bankseats.

cross both existing and new carriageway layouts. To minimize the overall span, abutments are placed as close to the operational carriageways as possible. This leads to very dominant end supports, which can be out of character in a rural environment. Large wingwalls can be disguised by realigning them parallel to the motorway or by screen planting. The latter, however, may not be effective at all times of the year. Three-span solutions can also be used, so that the abutments are less intrusive, but the side spans are likely to be short compared to the central span, and this can lead to lack of proportion and possible difficulties with uplift at the abutments.

19.6 Similarly for parallel widening schemes, one long span will be needed to cross the existing carriageway and a second span for the parallel carriageway. The longer span may be 40m or more in length, whereas the second span only needs to satisfy the clearance requirements for a single carriageway. If minimum clearances are adopted, this can lead to very unbalanced spans, which can be disconcerting in appearance, especially on high skew bridges. Parallel widening also leaves a large space through the longer span, which may not be occupied by carriageway and can be used for landscaping, screening or planting. This treatment needs to be handled with care, especially if asymmetric spans are adopted. As the planting matures, the unbalanced spans may be further exaggerated by one end of the bridge ending on a solid abutment, with the other merging with trees or vegetation. A more balanced span arrangement can be achieved using bankseats set back, rather than full-height abutments placed

The Appearance of Bridges and Other Highway Structures
Chapter 19 Bridges over widened motorways
FUNCTIONS OF BRIDGES & PARTICULAR FORMS THUS GENERATED

19.8a (left)
M1/A42
Junction.
High parapet
with short
cantilever
creates
dominant,
heavy
appearance.

close to the carriageways. Planting and earth moulding can also be used to give the appearance of symmetry, with similar treatment to each end of the bridge.

19.7 For some primary routes, the possibility of providing additional traffic capacity in the future after the initial widening must not be prevented. This is necessary if traffic growth within the design life of the bridge renders the carriageway width or bridge spans inadequate. Consequently, it is preferable to incorporate flexibility into the design by limiting the number of obstructions caused by piers or abutments. Current policy advises that bridge spans ought to be capable of accepting an additional lane on each carriageway. For parallel widening, use of the original carriageway may be retained in order to provide lane capacity during maintenance.

19.8 It is thus clear that long spans will be needed that can be quickly constructed using prefabricated beam elements in order to limit traffic disruption. Usually bridge beams must be installed during limited night-time road closures. Recent schemes have generally incorporated fabricated steel sections or precast prestressed concrete beams, although lightweight fabricated deck structures also have potential. For simple spans, the depth of these sections can be significant due to the long spans involved. Constant-depth beams are usually adopted, but steel solutions can incorporate variable-depth sections, giving a more pronounced camber if

desired. The opening through the span will appear as a wide slot with a potentially heavy deck looming over it. This effect can be mitigated in a number of ways:
- by increasing the clearance height
- by reducing the structural depth
- by using variable-depth beams
- by using a cross-section, which makes the real depth impossible to read.

Trapezoidal and curved sections have been used successfully by emphasizing a light-coloured fascia beam over a structure which is cast in shadow by a large edge cantilever; the use of a dark colour for the main structure can have similar effects, but some cantilever is still necessary. The first three methods are real solutions which alter the ratio of solid to void. The last two are visual effects which can minimize the appearance of depth, although they do not work in all lighting conditions because they do not change the silhouette. Actual construction of superstructures which incorporate some or all of these features may not be possible in all cases, and must be assessed against the construction restraints. The construction of very wide edge cantilevers is not always practical in construction terms, but total absence of any cantilever can lead to the main beams becoming very dominant.

PICTURE CREDITS
19.4b d WS Atkins; ph Arup. **19.5a d** Sir William Halcrow & Partners; ph Arup. **19.5b d** Howard Humphries; ph Arup. **19.6a d** Howard Humphries; ph Arup. **19.6b d**/ph Arup. **19.8a** ph Arup.

Chapter 20

Materials, finishes and detailing

20.1 The choice of type, variety and finish of the materials for bridges (and other highway structures) has a great bearing on the quantity and quality of detail of a structure and hence its scale. This, together with the inherent appearance of the material, is one of the most important fundamental factors in the appearance of bridges.

20.2 *The choice of materials and finish should depend on the context and setting of the bridge, and whether the bridge or other structure should relate to the road or to the adjacent environment.* Generally, the context has more influence on the finish and the choice of materials for cladding and for existing items, rather than for the prime structural elements.

20.3 The choice of materials and finishes affects the appearance of the structure in three different ways:
● the surface finish at both a visual and tactile level
● the junction of materials
● the number of different materials used in the structure.

20.4 The surface finish can vary from the bland, such as the smooth, grey, in situ concrete from a plain shutter, to extremes of the colourful and hand-crafted, like painted and gilded cast iron. Desire for surface texture, colour, natural colour variation, a cast texture or modelling, a carved or applied craft finish, a pattern or a particular tactile quality or sheen all require a particular choice of materials. To resort to imitating the appearance of one material with another, e.g. rubber shutter lining to imitate natural rubble stonework with in situ concrete, tends to show that the wrong material has been chosen to achieve the necessary effect. However, the imitation of unnatural treatments, such as baroque stonework, in another material can work well when treated sufficiently boldly (see Fig. 20.21a).

20.5 The junction of materials, i.e. the detailing, should express how the joint works and the nature of the materials. Honesty and simplicity are the fundamentals to be sought, but a great deal of effort is required to make details appear simple and effortless. If a detail looks complex, it generally means that it has not been thought out fully. Adding unnecessary detail to express a junction or fixing is unnecessary and inappropriate on bridges.

20.6 The number of different materials used should be kept to a minimum, except where a greater quantity of detail is required for visual reasons, and there is no scope for using a more visually complex form of structure, e.g. a truss or a masonry arch. A different material should be used for a distinct part of the structure, like a beam or abutment or parapet. The break between one material and another should be kept visually clear and crisp. For instance, where a masonry causeway with a masonry parapet changes to a steel bridge with a steel parapet, the material of the parapet should change at the change in structure.

As a corollary to this, where it is desirable to express that something is continuous where it is hidden, e.g. a bridge deck bearing on a bankseat, the parapet in this case should continue beyond the actual deck structure. The visual change should be where the element of the structure appears to end – an aesthetic decision, not a structural one.

20.7 The selection of materials and hence the details *depends on what is trying to be achieved visually.* If sleek elegance and crispness of detail are required to give expression to the dynamic flow and speed of traffic, one set of materials and details might be chosen; but if the aim is to fit the structure unobtrusively into an existing environment for

20.5a (above) Passerelle Pas Du Lac, St Quentin-en-Yvelines, France: over-expressed details.

20.6a (right) Shaldon Bridge, Devon. Change in parapet should coincide with change in structure as here.

the sake of stationary views, then a different set of materials and details might be chosen to express craftsmanship, vernacular detail and local geology.

IN SITU CONCRETE

20.8 The heavy appearance of mass concrete contrasting with lighter members elsewhere in the structure can, perhaps, be emphasized with advantage in the surface treatment. For mass concrete arches the heavy form should be expressed. Horizontal recesses or tile creasing courses can be used to express and neaten lift marks on mass concrete abutments and walls. Radial recesses or tile creasing may be useful to neaten the voussoir shapes created by the crack former for in situ arches.

20.9 Reinforced concrete, with its ability to take tension, offers opportunity for exploiting the quality of slenderness. *Sharpness of definition, conducive to a feeling of crispness, is the effect to be aimed at*; this will tend to be lost if too much use is made of rounded sections. With the thinner members used in such structures and the added subtlety of line, it becomes especially important to ensure that there is no distortion resulting from inadequate design of the bracing or support of the formwork.

20.10 Smooth concrete surfaces show up any staining, and special measures are desirable to render it less conspicuous, particularly on broader surfaces, which in any case are more difficult to make perfectly smooth.

20.11 The range of smooth, textured and profiled finishes in general use is as follows:
- plain concrete
- grooved
- sawn board
- knocked-off rib
- shutter liner
- exposed aggregate.

The most satisfactory textures in concrete are those which, in common with natural materials, have a small-scale and irregular pattern raised on the surface, like split, sawn or tooled stone, or timber. The least satisfactory are patterns that appear to have been stamped into the surface by a machine in regular geometrical shapes.

20.12 *Plain concrete* is classified as follows:

- F2 plain concrete with minimal blemishes
- F3 plain concrete with no blemishes whatsoever
- F4 plain concrete with no blemishes but boltholes filled with recessed filling.

20.12a (below) KINGSGATE FOOTBRIDGE, Durham: elegantly detailed plain concrete.

20.8a (top) TWICKENHAM BRIDGE, Middlesex: showing use of tile creasing to mark concrete lifts.

20.8b (above) TWICKENHAM BRIDGE, Middlesex: detail of pleasant texture of tile creasing.

20.13a (left) Avenue de Chartres Bridge, Chichester: ornamental use of grooves near slow-moving urban traffic.

20.13b (left) Humber Bridge. Ribbed anchor block emphasizes strength and mass.

20.14a (below, centre) Coventry Polytechnic. Sawn-board finish looks good in the sun.

20.14b (below) South Bank Arts Centre, London. Two-dimensional geometry helps sawn-board finish.

20.12b (above) Stadelhofen Undercroft, Zürich: sculptural concrete.

20.14c (above) A23 Bridge, Brighton Bypass. The knocked tooth has given a repeating pattern, and the facets are too wide.

20.14d (left) A40 Over Bridge, Gloucester. Rounded columns are best, using single narrow boards.

20.13 Grooved finish has chamfered sides to ease removal from shuttering, and is best used vertically to encourage channelling of rainwater or seepage. The depth of projection and module of grooved finishes can vary. Diagonal and horizontal grooves can be used for effect, but weathering is erratic and generally poor. The effect can be ribbed or a series of module markers, depending on centres.

20.14 Sawn-board finish is best where the boards are defined. This can be by varying board thickness to give a step, by using battens to form a groove or by rough sawing to expose the grain. The saw marks are of as much importance as the wood grain. Occasional knocked teeth on a band saw can be used to enhance the rough texture, but care should then be taken to avoid a repeating pattern. Boards can vary in width depending on the project: the narrower the board, the smaller the scale of the texture. On circular faceted columns, each facet should be a single board, and the narrower the better. Tapered columns or piers can be easily formed by cutting planks along their length at a slight angle to the sides, to give tapered boards.

The object is not to imitate wood but to give a texture to the concrete surface; sandblasting of the timber formwork to expose the grain tends to give too great an imitation of timber on the concrete surface. Steps between the boards or recesses can help to modulate the surface. Sawn-board finish is also excellent for complex geometric surfaces.

20.15 Knocked-off rib finish is commonly known as 'elephant house' finish, since it was most famously used for the Elephant House at London Zoo. The cast ribs must be knocked off by hand with a hammer, and it is important for the workman to practice beforehand and get a rhythm of blows alternating from left and right. The effect should be of rough ribs exposing the aggregate, not of a rib with lumps knocked out. Rubber moulds to imitate this are ineffective, since no aggregate is exposed and there are no sharp arrises. The ribs should be vertical, though the surface can be battered, since it is important to avoid shadow effects from unwashed areas. Surfaces curved in plan exploit this finish well, enhancing the rugged effect at corners.

20.14e (right) Stadelhofen Station, Zürich. Three-dimensional geometry is helped by sawn-board finish.

20.14f (far right) St Gotthard Pass 'Hairpin' Bridge, Switzerland: circular column with fine board-marking and lifts expressed.

20.15a (left) Elephant House, London Zoo. Rough texture developed for elephants to rub looks good, especially on curved walls.

20.15b (above) Pen y Clip Tunnel, North Wales. Bold geometry helps knocked-off rib finish.

20.16a (far left) York Bypass. Modelled ribs of shutter liner give interest.

20.16b (left) Alma Station Viaduct, Brussels, Belgium: bark-textured columns – high visual interest.

20.17b (below) Precast Wall, Mecca, Saudi Arabia: smooth and sandblasted finishes to give Islamic patterns.

20.17a (right) Precast Pier, Narborough, Leicestershire: light acid wash, and light sandblast on base and fins.

20.18a (right) Stadelhofen Wall, Zürich: module derived from lifts and movement joints.

20.16 Shutter liner finish is generally produced by using proprietary rubber liners, which give a vast variety of ornamental modelling to plain concrete surfaces. There is no exposure of aggregate. Generally, the more repetitive the pattern the more it tends inappropriately to look like wallpaper. Imitations of natural materials such as stone, brick, slates or wood should generally be avoided since the colour is wrong, they do not weather like the real article, and there is no microtexture. It is best to use a specific ornamental pattern designed for and celebrating the material, and designed with the whole wall in mind. Alternatively, a number of different textures can be used to create patterns. Occasionally, a more bold use of deliberately outrageous false effects such as logs, bark or bamboo might be used if designed by a talented architect or artist.

20.17 Exposed aggregate finishes give a very wide range of appearances – depending on the method and depth of exposure – varying from light acid washing for a finish similar to dressed portland stone, to heavy retarder and grit blasting to give a finish similar to pebble dashing. The colour and the texture, important from a distance and close to respectively, are affected by the size, shape and colour of the coarse and fine aggregates and the cement, and by the degree of exposure. Very slight differences in exposure can have a considerable difference in appearance, as the cement and aggregate change their dominance. Careful control and supervision are vital. Exposed aggregates to finishes are much easier to control under the factory conditions of precasting.

Bush-hammering and other tool working are also possible, but are labour intensive. For practical reasons, and to preserve sharpness of definition, it is generally undesirable to take any rough finish to the extreme edge of a plane surface.

20.18b (below) Biasca Viaduct, Switzerland. Board and lift marking give scale.

20.21a (below) Eiffel Tower, Paris: bold precast concrete cladding to abutments.

20.25a (above) Shaldon Bridge, Teignmouth, Devon: precast rings as permanent shuttering.

20.25b (left) Touche Bridge, Toulouse, France: precast columns with tiles to mask the joint with in situ deck.

20.18 Concrete surfaces usually require vertical joints between one pour and the next, and often horizontal joints as well between one lift and the next. These joints give a basic grid. The practicable intervals between them, dictated by formwork material sizes, produce a convincing and appropriate scale, and the positions of both vertical and horizontal lines can usually be adjusted to make a balanced system. The joints may be made almost invisible by taping between the shutters, or they may be emphasized by being given a deep 'V'. The vertical may be suppressed and the horizontal exaggerated or vice versa as appropriate to the particular circumstances. If precast facing panels are to be used in conjunction with in situ work, the panels should bear some relation in layout and size to the natural basic grid referred to above. Recessed joints normally give an impression of greater strength than raised joints.

20.19 On fascias and other vertical surfaces exposed to weather, fluting or vertical tooling will help to canalize rainwater and thus provide a pattern to be emphasized rather than spoiled by weathering. A backfall on deck edge upstands is important to limit dirt-laden water running down any fascia. Care must be taken to avoid any rustable fixings.

20.20 See Chapter 29, Paragraph 29.23, for further information on retaining walls.

Precast Concrete

20.21 Precast concrete is commonly used for bridge elements, e.g. beams, columns, deck edges, parapets and barriers; for cladding of abutments, walls or whole bridges; and for elements of proprietary retaining wall systems. Whole bridges are occasionally precast, especially footbridges. *The high-quality modelling and surface detail possible in precast concrete ought to be exploited when opportunities arise to use it.*

20.22 Cladding is covered in Chapter 29, Paragraph 29.33, proprietary wall systems in Chapter 29, Paragraphs 29.18, 29.19 and 29.22.

20.23 Precast deck edges permit adjustment to produce a sweet line along the deck, and to overcome tolerance in deck construction needed for glued cantilever construction, long viaducts and all bridges when viewed obliquely (see Fig. 6.29a).

20.24 Precast beams, whilst practical, are not generally beautiful in themselves. A long cantilever helps their elevational appearance by keeping them in shadow. They are generally most noticeable on the bridge soffit, where they should be arranged in an orderly manner. If the bridge tapers or curves in plan, the plan arrangement of the precast beams needs to be carefully considered. A simple linear arrangement of beams with, preferably full depth, in situ concrete to form the taper or edge curve is usually best.

20.25 Precast columns, either complete or as rings for permanent shuttering, can have advantages, especially where access is difficult due to tides or traffic. The junction with in situ work needs to be carefully handled. Ceramic tiles have been used to mark the junction successfully.

METALS

20.26 *Steel is best detailed to be simple, crisp and to express clarity of purpose* (see Fig. 15.2b).

20.27 Where plate girders are used, the clean appearance of welding is generally preferable to bolted connections, and this is further improved by omitting stiffeners on the outside face. However, bolted fixings and stiffeners can sometimes add useful detail to give scale and emphasis.

20.28 It is important that a suitable colour be chosen for painting steel bridges. A uniform colour throughout is usually best. If it is necessary to emphasize one part of the structure, for example to distinguish the main span from an approach viaduct where they are not already clearly enough distinguished by their size or form, some contrast in colour may be useful, but needs very careful handling (see also Chapter 21). Galvanizing weathers to a pleasant matt grey, which looks good with concrete.

20.29 Steel is excellent for simple straight structures, but where the structure curves on plan, the beams should follow the curvature rather than be faceted.

20.30 *Weathering steel has the advantage of not needing painting, but it has other problems, which can be largely overcome by careful detailing.* In principle, no water must flow from the steel onto any other surface, especially concrete, and in particular when the steel is fresh and still forming its first oxidization. Water must not be trapped in pockets. All surfaces must clearly drain away to a safe area. Drips are needed on the underside of beams, with trays over columns and abutments to collect the water. Concrete should be carefully wrapped in waterproof sheeting to protect it during construction, once the steel is installed. Nothing must be attached to the surface of the steel during construction – no painted signs or numbers, no sticky labels, no chalk or wax crayon marks (since these will retard the oxidization in that area, and get worse with time). Colours can be a wide range of browns to almost black. They can be determined with the manufacturer but are still subject

20.27a (below) ALMA BRIDGE, Paris: clean appearance of welded beam with no stiffeners.

20.27b (right) CAR PARK BRIDGE, Swindon, Wiltshire: interesting support but cumbersome heavy deck due to stiffeners.

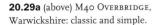
20.29a (above) M40 OVERBRIDGE, Warwickshire: classic and simple.

20.29b (right) SOUTH QUAY VIADUCT, Docklands Light Railway, London. Beams should follow curve of deck, not be faceted.

20.32a (right) LEITH, Edinburgh: modern craft blacksmith work in mild steel.

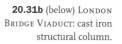

20.31a (below) PONT D'ARCOLE, Paris: cast iron lamp column.

20.31b (below) LONDON BRIDGE VIADUCT: cast iron structural column.

to variation due to site conditions. Specialist advice for the use of weathering steel should be sought from the manufacturer. It should not be used where the public may brush against it, and it should not have junctions with painted steel due to problems of repainting. It can work well with timber parapets, particularly for footbridges (see Fig. 12.34a).

20.31 Cast iron was once common for bridge structures but is generally now only used for ornamental street furniture, drainageware and restoration work. Spheroidal cast iron is stronger and less brittle than traditional grey cast iron, and therefore can be particularly useful in strengthening old bridges. *Crispness of detail, complexity of surface form and craftsmanship in mould manufacture are the key to high-quality cast iron work.* The designer should work closely with the foundryman to exploit the material correctly. Slightly rough sand-casting finish and inherent slight imperfections are characteristic of cast iron. Visually, painting (with possibly a sprayed zinc coating) is better than epoxy powder coating, since the latter masks the texture and can make the object look like plastic. Cast steel may have a future for columns.

20.32 Historically, wrought iron was used until the mass production of steel in the 1880s. It is now only available for restoration work through museums. It appears more fibrous than steel or cast iron, especially when it rusts. *Due to its different visual quality, it should, if possible, be preserved, especially where visible, during restoration work on historic bridges.* Due to its high malleability, it should be used for restoring

ornamental gates and lamp brackets, etc., if they are of wrought iron on a historic structure. Modern 'wrought iron' used for street furniture is actually steel, though craftsmanship can still produce excellent modern results.

20.33 Stainless steel is generally only used for handrails on prestigious structures and for fixings on small cable structures. The finish can be polished, peened to give a matt effect or brushed to give directional matt effect.

20.34 Aluminium is rarely used for bridge structures but is very common for parapets and other street furniture. Its natural oxidized grey colour and matt appearance, once weathered, look excellent with concrete. It is not usually necessary to use coloured anodizing or powder coating to protect it. Its light weight makes it suitable for sign gantries, etc., especially when cantilevered, but its lower strength than steel often requires larger box sections, e.g. for lighting columns, which can make them appear bulky in comparison to steel ones. It can often be used most efficiently in conjunction with steel or concrete, where the different loadings in the parts can be expressed in the various materials.

20.35 Bronze is excellent for high-quality handrails and ornamental castings, where its natural patina burnished by handling gives a very beautiful and long-lasting appearance. It needs no finishing and improves in appearance with age. Unfortunately it gets stolen by vandals, as does aluminium.

20.36 Gold leaf may be used where a gold colour is required on ornamental details, especially lettering and particularly on historic bridges. It should be used extremely sparingly. The resistance to corrosion ensures great longevity of appearance without deterioration, and is therefore good value for money. It contrasts well with stone, concrete and painted metal.

MASONRY

20.37 Stone is covered in Chapters 3, 5 and 29. The variation in colour within a type of stone and between individual adjacent stones adds to its beauty and should be exploited. Decoration is probably best avoided in modern bridges, but where there is some pattern it should repeat, based on the actual stone size rather than a predimensioned module. Any lettering is best carved into the stonework rather than applied.

Facing slabs in materials like granite, slate or marble generally come in larger sizes and more regular shapes than loadbearing stone, and are generally cut and dressed to exploit the pattern and grain within the stone. This visual difference to loadbearing stone should be expressed, and contrasts of colour, texture and surface pattern can be exploited. Generally, the coarser the surface texture, the larger the apparent scale of the masonry. Stone which is heavily figured or with a strong directional grain needs careful consideration to slab orientation. Book matching and quartering will generally give an appearance too opulent and grandiose for a bridge. Stone paving comes as slabs, kerbs and setts, and many types and colours are available. It is hard wearing, improves with age and looks excellent, so is very suitable for high-quality pedestrian areas. The paving design should be part of the overall landscape design by the landscape architect. Stone can work well with gravel, concrete paving and brick.

20.37a (right) EGTON BRIDGE, North Yorkshire: detail showing 3-D modelling of cutwater.

20.36a (above) VAUXHALL BRIDGE, London: gold leaf for lettering on granite.

20.37c (above) MAIN SQUARE, San Marino: stone and brick paving.

20.37b (right) LOIRE BRIDGE, Saumur, France. Note the colour variation, pattern on stone module and incised lettering.

20.38b (left) EVRY CATHEDRAL, France: well-modelled acoustic brick wall.

20.38a (below) RAILWAY VIADUCT, Staples Corner, North London: traditional brick detailing.

20.38d (left) HEMBRUGSTRAAT, Amsterdam: virtuoso brickwork.

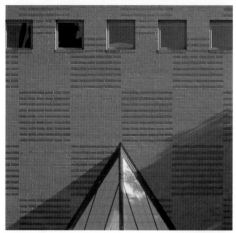

20.38c (above) SEWARD HEDGES SCHOOL, Chicago, USA: bold, modern brickwork.

20.38e (right) MACERATA, Italy: high, craft quality classical brickwork.

20.38f (far right) BOUNDARY WALL, East India Docks, London: excellent simple grandeur of battered and buttressed dock wall.

20.39b (left)
CROSSPOINT
BUSINESS
PARK, Rugby,
Northamptonshire:
blockwork
and brickwork
combined in wall.

20.39a (above)
CHAPEL WALL,
Guildford,
Surrey: concrete
blockwork with
knapped
flint surface.

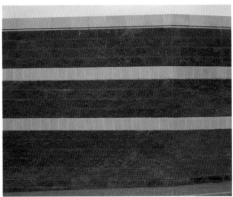

20.38 Brick and its usage is covered in Chapters 3 and 29. Although it can be structural, it is now generally used for facing. Great variations of colour, texture, sheen and tonal modulation are possible, within and between bricks, so it is best to specify two or three acceptable bricks for each type with a specific acceptance for equivalents, samples of which must be submitted and accepted prior to tender. This ensures that a visually acceptable brick is supplied, and simplifies what is acceptable for contractors and suppliers. Bricks with an applied surface texture, e.g. sand-faced, weather less well than integrally coloured and textured bricks in the harsh environmental conditions of a road, and cannot withstand frost or impact damage without spoiling the appearance. Glazed bricks can, however, add a useful bright and bold colour contrast, and are good in limited quantities where damage by impact is unlikely. It is generally best to use a brick type which matches one locally used, if one is dominant, and then select contrasting sorts as appropriate. Local details such as tile creasing, precast art deco keystones, in set flints, ornamental dentil courses or diaper-work can be utilized effectively to make brickwork suit the locality. Modelling is best very deep and bold to give good shadow line. An architect should generally be used to detail brickwork, particularly where it is ornamental. Whilst traditional 'vernacular' details can be used, contemporary designs are to be encouraged. Recent studies have shown that loadbearing brickwork parapets may often be structurally adequate (when at least $1\frac{1}{2}$ bricks thick), and can have great visual advantages over other standard parapets, due to variations in pattern, modelling, texture and colour.

20.39c (above, left) LIMEHOUSE LINK, East London: polished red and rough-split white blockwork.

20.40a (above) NORTH AMERICAN BURR TRUSS: standard construction in forested areas until the 1960s.

20.40b (left) BROCKING BRIDGE, Surrey: detail of bolted junction of members (see also 25.7a).

20.39 Concrete blockwork is covered largely in Chapter 29. Its variety of surface finish, texture and colour – in particular warm stone colours – its large scale, and its ease of incorporation with other masonry such as brick and precast concrete, can all be exploited.

TIMBER, PLASTICS AND GLASS

20.40 Timber has increasing usage for footbridges (see Chapters 7 and 12, Paragraphs 12.33–12.35, and *Footbridges in the Countryside* by the Countryside Commission for Scotland) and possibly for parapets, but its main usage is for environmental barriers and fences. Large-span timber bridges were common in Canada and the USA until the 1960s but are rare in the UK. *Timber comes*

20.40c (left) SHIPLAKE WEIR BRIDGE, Oxfordshire: simple timber bridge.

20.40d (below, left) TIMBER WALKWAY, Fox Lake, USA. Timber fits well into the natural environment.

20.41a (below) FOOTBRIDGE, Shank Castle, Cumbria: all-plastic construction unfortunately imitating traditional forms.

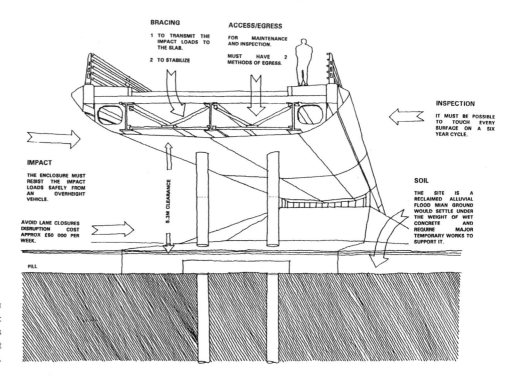

BRACING
1 TO TRANSMIT THE IMPACT LOADS TO THE SLAB.
2 TO STABILIZE

ACCESS/EGRESS
FOR MAINTENANCE AND INSPECTION.
MUST HAVE 2 METHODS OF EGRESS.

INSPECTION
IT MUST BE POSSIBLE TO TOUCH EVERY SURFACE ON A SIX YEAR CYCLE.

IMPACT
THE ENCLOSURE MUST RESIST THE IMPACT LOADS SAFELY FROM AN OVERHEIGHT VEHICLE.

AVOID LANE CLOSURES DISRUPTION COST APPROX £50 000 PER WEEK.

5.3M CLEARANCE

SOIL
THE SITE IS A RECLAIMED ALLUVIAL FLOOD MIAN GROUND WOULD SETTLE UNDER THE WEIGHT OF WET CONCRETE AND REQUIRE MAJOR TEMPORARY WORKS TO SUPPORT IT.

FILL

20.41b (right) SECOND SEVERN CROSSING APPROACH BRIDGES: plastic cladding. Cladding is fundamental to the design, not an afterthought.

20.42a (bottom) Pont de l'Alma, Paris: glass balustrade.

20.41c (below) Poole Bridge Competition Design, Dorset: cable net bridge using innovative carbon fibre cables and an innovative form.

20.42b (below) Quai de l'Hôtel de Ville, Paris. Glazing under footbridge ramp protects riverside park from noise.

in relatively short lengths and in limited cross-section, and although they can be increased by laminating, these factors should be visible as a fundamental part of the design. Although in the past timber was cut away to produce very elegant joints, it is now more structurally efficient and logical to bolt members together. The correct types of glues and metal fixings are critical to durability.

20.41 Plastics are starting to be used for bridges (see Fig. 9.6a), and can be employed for decks, columns, cable cladding and balustrades. Where they are extruded or pultruded, there will be a constant cross-section, and construction can be similar to that for timber, although the cross-sectional crushing strength of the hollow sections needs different fixing details. *With any new material, it is vital to work with the best and most talented architect or product designer to get acceptable visual results if the material, though innovative in itself, is not to be condemned due to its appearance; innovative appearance should go hand-in-hand with innovative technology.* Plastics are best used where they have a specific advantage in a particular situation, e.g. for lightness in an inaccessible location, or for high stiffness-to-weight ratio for certain claddings. Good results often come from using new technology such as plastics in combination with other more familiar materials. The material should be appropriate to its function. (Plastic glazing is covered in Chapter 12, Paragraph 12.42.)

20.42 Glass is used for balustrades (see Fig. 12.33a), environmental barriers and cladding of footbridges (see Chapter 12, Paragraph 12.42). Since glass is almost invariably to be seen through, clear untinted glass is generally best in the UK climate. Where clarity is not required, as at edges or to mask fixings or dirt splashing, fritted line tones or dot matrix graduated tones can be used (see Fig. 12.40b). Toughened laminated glass is usually best to minimize damage and dangerous subsequent shards. Glass is generally preferable to plastics for glazing, since it is non-yellowing, scratch-resistant and non-flammable.

Chapter 21

Colour

21.1 Colour is an important part of beauty. St Thomas Aquinas said: 'For beauty there are three requirements. Firstly a certain wholeness or perfection, for whatever is incomplete is ugly; secondly a due proportion or harmony; and thirdly clarity, so that brightly coloured things are called beautiful.' *It is therefore important to remember that the purpose of colour is to elucidate form.*

21.4a (right) ST GOTTHARD VIADUCT, Switzerland. Dark balustrade disappears against rocks or trees.

21.2 Many materials are self-coloured and only have a small range of tone within that colour, i.e. in situ concrete, galvanized steel, aluminium and micaceous iron oxide paint for steel. The natural colour of all these is grey, so in the majority of situations colours will be limited to a range of greys. In the past, many paint systems were restricted in colour to greys, but with modern manufacturing methods there is now no such limitation.

21.3 With both the typical British overcast sky and the distance at which bridges are often seen, especially in rural areas, perception of colour reduces so that all tends to grey; brighter colours, therefore, are of little benefit generally. Greens and pale yellows lose their colour quickest with distance, whereas reds, oranges and reddish-yellows can retain their colour when seen from many miles away.

21.4 In rural areas it is generally not intended to draw attention to the highway structures unless they are exceptional (see Chapter 2); for this purpose neutral colours like greys are usually better than bright ones. If there are special considerations which call for inconspicuousness, a dark tone will help, especially if the structure is seen against a dark background such as trees, buildings or a hillside; if inconspicuousness against the sky is required, a lighter tone

is better. This is particularly important where the balustrade needs to be inconspicuous, which is usually the case (see Paragraph 21.13).

21.5 On concrete bridges, metal balustrades, even though they may sometimes introduce a note of gaiety, should be painted in colours that are related to the neutral and warm greys of the concrete surfaces.

21.6 On steel bridges, the colour of the balustrades should similarly be related to the colour selected for the outside faces of the main steelwork.

21.7 The impression of lightness in a parapet can be emphasized if desired by painting it a much paler tone than the rest of the structure.

21.4b (below) M40, Buckinghamshire. Light balustrade disappears against the sky.

21.6a (above) DOCKLANDS LIGHT RAILWAY, Canary Wharf. Balustrade matches blue structural steel.

21.10a (above) M6, Lancashire: successful use of colour in a low-key landscape.

21.11b (below) SFALASSA BRIDGE, Southern Italy. Colour exploits strong sunlight and a dramatic location.

21.11c (below, centre) WATERLOO EAST RAIL AND FOOTBRIDGES. Bright bridges enhance townscape.

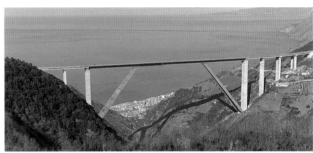

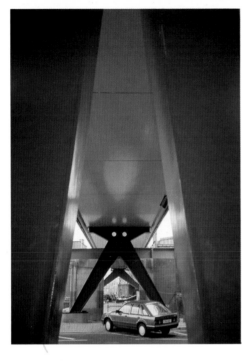

21.11a (right) WATERLOO EAST FOOTBRIDGE, London: bold colour in a rundown location.

21.11d (left) FESTIVAL PARK FLYOVER, Stoke-on-Trent. Colour used as part of festival concept.

21.8 Variation and contrast of tone can often be of more lasting interest than a splash of colour. Monochrome schemes making use of warm and cool neutral shades, from black or charcoal to white or off-white, look very well, provided contrasts are sharp and definitive. The concrete colour itself can be made part of such a scheme by the use of dark and light aggregate, black, normal and white cement, and various combinations. Normally the light tones, being more prominent, are used for the deck edge and fascias, the recessed beams, like the columns supporting the deck, being kept dark in contrast. This emphasizes the natural effect of shadows and light. Dark tones make soffits appear lower (see Chapters 11 and 16).

21.9 Both black and white are best given a very slight bias, black towards blue and white towards cream. More generally, a greyish colour is most useful, since it will go well both with natural surroundings at all seasons and with most ordinary building materials. But here again, an absolutely neutral grey is apt to look dead and dingy. A bias towards blue, green, red or yellow is desirable, the actual choice depending on the surroundings. A bluish-grey or reddish-grey is perhaps more appropriate in a sophisticated architectural setting than in open country. A dark purple-grey is a more accurate colour for false shadows, especially in bright sunlight.

21.10 There are situations where it is possible and desirable to use colours other than greys on bridges. Colour can be introduced with the following materials: painted steel, painted galvanized steel (for street furniture), precast concrete (not structural beams), masonry facings (mainly for abutments), plastic claddings and barriers.

21.11 *The use of bright colour would only be desirable in two basic situations:*
(a) *where the bridge should be a bold statement* (see Chapter 2, Paragraph 2.3)
(b) *in an urban situation*, especially where there is an overall strategy for townscape colour schemes, including architecture, street furniture and bridges (see Fig. 13.3a).
In such situations the use of colour should be considered, but it may well not be desirable.

21.13b (right) A13 Pɪᴘᴇ Bʀɪᴅɢᴇ, London Docklands. Colour enhances the bold form in the docks environment.

21.13a (above) Tʀᴀɴsᴘᴏʀᴛ Iɴᴛᴇʀᴄʜᴀɴɢᴇ, Cʜᴜʀ, Switzerland: metallic colour for steel with boldly coloured balustrade.

21.13c (left) Bʀᴏᴄᴋʟᴇʏ Jᴀᴄᴋ Fᴏᴏᴛʙʀɪᴅɢᴇ, Lewisham, London: bold colour of painted steel.

21.15a (above) Vᴀᴜxʜᴀʟʟ Bʀɪᴅɢᴇ, London: historic colour scheme for old bridge.

21.12 When bold or unusual use of colour is proposed, a mock-up length of handrail or panel in wood should be set up on the site, painted with alternative colours and viewed from a distance to make final judgement.

21.13 The prime function of paint on steel is to protect the metal. There are few instances where a contrast of colours is desirable, a single colour or a group of related tones of the same colour being generally preferable. Very occasionally, where the design of the bridge is good enough and the landscape can take it, a single bold colour is successful, but more often it will be wise to relate rather than contrast bridge and background. Strong shades of green are considered by some to clash with vegetation, and care must be taken when using them in rural situations. 'Metallic' colours from bronze-green to copper and silver grey can look well on steel structures.

If it is desired to call attention to a bridge, for example a well-designed ornamental footbridge in a public park or a pedestrian bridge over a busy road, where usage is to be encouraged by making the bridge prominent, a contrast with the background in tone or colour is desirable (see Fig. 12.2a). White is often very effective, as is the traditional bright Chinese red. Blue is also a traditional and satisfactory colour, which looks good against the cold greys of an English sky.

In special situations like docks, and amongst large engineering works where bold, even fluorescent colours are used on other engineering installations such as cranes or oil rigs, similar high-visibility colour schemes can be used on suitable bridges (see Fig. 2.20a). However, such colour schemes should only proceed with the utmost care and consideration.

Shades of greens and browns are very useful where a bold colour is not suitable and the drabness of grey is not sought.

21.14 *Street furniture such as balustrades and lampposts should not be painted in a colour intended to draw attention away from the form of the bridge*, which should be the dominant aspect of the design. Where, however, a single design of bridge is to be repeated many times, as on a motorway, occasional variations in the treatment of parapet colour can help to obviate monotony. But the use of fancy patterns or bold colours is seldom successful.

21.15 On historic bridges it is generally best to use the original historic colour scheme, where this can be found from archives or by taking samples. Historically, the range of pigments available before the late 19th century was very limited. Specialist advice should be sought (see also Chapters 22 and 26). New bridges or street furniture near historic bridges may also benefit from the historic colour scheme, e.g. the black and white of canal livery.

21.16 The colouring of precast concrete by pigments has in the past been unreliable and unpredictable, both visually and chemically. Choice of colour was thus limited to that available through natural aggregates and grey or white cement. Even this opportunity was little exploited. Recent developments in more stable inorganic pigments, more thorough mixing in the dry state rather than the wet mix, and much improved quality control systems, have made the use of coloured concrete more reliable and practical. Since only the surface is required to be of the desired colour, the use of in situ coloured structural concrete still tends to be uneconomic and unreliable, except by exposed aggregate techniques (see Chapter 20). Coloured in situ concrete for hard landscape paving has potential in certain circumstances.

21.16a (below) Mission City Centre, Canada: coloured in situ concrete paving.

21.17 Concrete colours reflecting natural stone or earth shades are usually most satisfactory, e.g. the warm yellows of Bath stone. Strong colours, especially blues, look strange and have a reputation for fading. As long as there is a surface treatment, the aggregate will almost always be the strongest contributor to the perceived colour; any pigment should be used to emphasize this natural colour. The type of surface treatment also is a strong determinant on the final appearance of colour. It is important to judge colour from a very large sample at a reasonable viewing distance. Small samples seen close to often appear very different.

21.17a (above) Vauxhall Bridge Underpass River Walk, London. Three colours of precast concrete plus natural slate and gravel give elegant hard landscaping.

21.17b (left) Newton Cap Viaduct, Co. Durham: precast parapet panel sample viewed at a distance.

21.18a (above) LIMEHOUSE LINK, London Docklands: dynamic use of coloured polished concrete.

21.18b (above, right) AVENUE DE CHARTRES FOOTBRIDGE, Chichester, West Sussex: coloured bricks utilizing contrast in sheen.

21.19a (above) BRITFORD NAVIGATION BRIDGE, Salisbury: traditional, elegant white painted timber railings.

21.18 Masonry facings in stone, brick or concrete blockwork give a large opportunity for colour, depending on the natural colour of the materials. The range of possibilities is very wide, and is covered in Chapters 23 and 29. Blue Staffordshire bricks, glazed bricks and polished concrete have particular potential for introducing colour into masonry facings.

21.19 Timber parapets are best self-coloured or painted white on traditional bridges where that is the traditional colour.

21.20 Where there are pipes, cables or other visually unwanted attachments on existing bridges, these are best painted the same colour as the background to camouflage them. The best colours for camouflage are light blue, grey, beige and mauve.

Chapter 22

Lighting

| **22.1** | *Lamp columns on bridges are best avoided, either by omitting the need for lighting or, on short-span bridges, by placing lighting columns beyond the ends of the bridge.* Modern lighting technology should be exploited to illuminate the bridge from beyond, even though this may not be the most efficient lighting. Catenary lighting may also avoid the need for columns on the bridge.

| **22.2** | Any street lighting equipment should be considered as an integral part of the aesthetic design. The height of the lighting columns, the appearance of any fixing corbels and the setting out of the lighting are the most critical factors.

| **22.3** | If the lamp standards are going to be a conspicuous feature in side views of the bridge, which is usually the case, it is better to site them on a central reservation, or to incorporate them as special features in the parapet. Here, however, the columns and light fittings may well need to be specially designed to suit the design of the bridge.

22.1a (right) PILAR BRIDGE, Zaragoza, Spain: high mast lighting to illuminate river bridge.

22.2a (below) EGAR (EASTERN GATEWAY APPROACH ROAD) APPROACH RAMPS, London Docklands: obtrusive corbels for light fittings.

22.3a (right) EGAR BRIDGE, London Docklands: lights as a feature of a civic bridge.

22.3b (far left) Customs Wharf Bridge, Leith: specially designed light fittings on urban bridge.

22.3c (left) River Thames Wall, Vauxhall, London: special cast iron lamp columns.

22.7a (below) Chertsey Bridge, Surrey. Additional short lamp columns were added when the bridge was restored.

22.4 On multi-span bridges, lighting columns should preferably be placed above structural piers or columns. If this is not possible, they should be placed symmetrical to the piers or columns and to the bridge. Lighting columns should not be placed staggered in plan over a bridge, unless the skew effectively gives staggered column or pier positions. On formal urban bridges, opposite pairs of lights can be an attractive feature.

22.5 When setting out the spacing of lighting columns along a length of road, they should start from the centre of the bridge or the bridge lighting positions if the bridge is asymmetrical, and then be equally spaced.

22.6 The daytime appearance of lighting installations should comply with *BS5489: Part 1: 1992, Chapter 5*.

Ornamental lamp columns designed specifically for a particular scheme as part of the architecture of the bridge may, however, benefit from having more of a sturdy monumental presence.

22.7 The lighting of old bridges raises different problems. Most old bridges, even when widened, are spoiled if tall modern lamp-standards are erected on them, except perhaps when they are in a central reservation. The possibility of short columns at closer intervals may well be considered in such cases, but the placing of any columns on the outer edge of the bridge should obviously be carefully related to the spacing of piers and abutments. If the overall length of the bridge is not too great, it is desirable to light from each end only, with an increased mounting height and stronger lamps.

22.8b (right) BEDFORD TOWN BRIDGE: unsympathetically modified lights of the 1960s.

22.8a (below) BEDFORD TOWN BRIDGE: original lights.

22.8c (top) TWICKENHAM BRIDGE, Middlesex: elegant original lighting.

22.10a (above) FRAMWELL GATE BRIDGE, Durham. Floodlighting also lights the pedestrian path.

22.9a (above) BLACKFRIARS BRIDGE, London: navigational lighting as an afterthought.

22.8 Where existing historic lampposts and lanterns are on an old bridge, they should be restored and reused. Where parts of the light fittings have been altered, e.g. extended columns or new lanterns, it is best to try to restore the light fittings back to their original appearance even though they may not be contemporary with the bridge. New lighting technology can be incorporated to bring lighting levels up to modern standards, but where this is in conflict with the historic appearance, the appearance should take precedence over achieving lighting levels. A combination of refurbished historic light fittings and remote floodlighting can produce good results.

22.9 Special lighting problems arise in connection with lights on bridges over railways and canals, and navigational lights on rivers. The former often have to be masked in order not to confuse train drivers and boatmen, which may make the lantern look peculiarly clumsy in the daytime. Any measures that can be taken, therefore, through careful planning of the installation to reduce such masking to a minimum will be well worthwhile.

Navigational lights are often completely ignored in the design of a new bridge and appear as an ill-considered afterthought; many London Thames bridges suffer in this way. Such eyesores should be avoided by collaboration at the outset between the authorities concerned.

22.10b (left) Southwark Street, London. Lights should be fixed to bridges where possible.

22.12a (bottom, left) Dornie Bridge, A87, West Highlands: lights incorporated in parapet for sensitive site.

22.15a (below) Transporter Bridge, Middlesbrough: excellent floodlighting on a historic bridge.

22.12 In special situations, particularly single carriageway bridges, lighting can be incorporated in the balustrade. This can be useful in special locations and on elevated slip road flyovers in multi-level free-flow junctions, where the highest bridge can be very prominent, and the lighting even more so.

22.13 In general, when bridges are seen against a background of trees or buildings, the lighting columns should be lower than the height of such trees or buildings, as is the recommendation for all lighting on roads.

22.14 The colour of the lighting columns, brackets and luminaires should comply with the advice in Chapter 21.

22.10 Often in the past, lighting below bridges has been ignored in the design of the bridge, but such provision may be necessary – essential in the case of lengthy underpasses – and it should be done in such a way as to produce a good appearance both by day and by night. If the surface of the structure is to be used for reflecting light, this should be borne in mind in considering its finish, (see Chapter 17 for tunnels).

Lamp columns placed below bridges look ridiculous and ill thought-out. The lamps should be fixed to the columns or soffit, with the necessary thought for the provision of wiring. Broad motorway bridges may need lighting permanently (see Chapter 11).

22.15 *Ornamental illumination or floodlighting of bridges at night, where appropriate, should emphasize the basic geometric form of the structure*, should utilize the necessary road lighting, and must avoid glare from the light fittings. A mixture of colours of light can help emphasize the various parts of the bridge. Care needs to be taken to avoid distorting the visual balance of the structure by over- or under-emphasizing certain parts. Multiple small light sources can be very effective and are more tunable. The daytime appearance of the fittings needs to be considered.

22.11 Lighting on suspension bridges, cable-stayed structures, through trusses and other bridges where the structure is above the deck should preferably be incorporated into the structural members or cables, or lighting columns placed to co-ordinate with them.

Chapter 23
Decoration and sculpture

23.1 Murals and other decoration on highway structures have a purpose, as does all true art. Art for art's sake is inappropriate in such public locations. *The purpose is to enhance the appearance of the structure, give it a more human and welcoming scale in relationship to its viewers, either pedestrians or vehicle users, and to discourage graffiti.*

23.2 Murals are used frequently on pedestrian underpasses and also occasionally on retaining walls and tunnels. Sculpture and coats of arms are occasionally used on bridge abutments, tunnel portals, etc., especially where a certain civic pride is called for.

23.3 Defacement by graffiti needs to be discouraged because:

- It spoils the appearance of the structure.
- It encourages racism and obscenity, which are unacceptable.
- It costs public money to remove it.
- The presence of graffiti is psychologically threatening, especially to the most vulnerable. This discourages people from using underpasses, which in turn encourages mugging, etc., in under-used underpasses and also increases the danger to pedestrians who prefer to cross a dangerous road rather than use a threatening underpass.

23.4 For these reasons, the art forms appropriate to bridges, underpasses and retaining walls are quite specific.

23.5 *For areas only seen at relatively high speed from a vehicle, bold abstract forms, strong textures or smooth surfaces, bright colours, strong tonal contrasts and simple geometries are usually best.*

23.2a (right) Blackwall Tunnel, London: simple decoration at portal.

23.5a (below) Euston Underpass, London: bold colour and geometry.

23.2b (above) Maidenhead Railway Bridge. The coat of arms adds nothing to this bridge.

23.5b (above) Cardiff Bay Link Road: bold idea and simple geometry for viewing from cars.

23.6a (right) WARWICK ROAD, Coventry: sculpted concrete with good close detail.

23.6c (far right) SCULPTURE BY JOAN MIRÓ, La Défense, Paris: suitable for vehicles and pedestrians.

23.6b (below) LABERAUDIE BRIDGE, Cahors, France: folk art decoration.

23.6 *Where the surface is seen by pedestrians, especially residents, from a distance as well as from vehicles, forms and colours may be less bold.* Natural earth colours are less wearing on the eye, and forms can be more complex and less abstract.

23.7 *Where the surface is seen close up by pedestrians, bold abstract forms are inappropriate.* Since they cannot be appreciated close to, they have less complexity to the eye, are less interesting, and hence less appreciated as art by the layperson. Also the large blank areas that they include encourage graffiti.

23.8 Where the surface is seen close up, therefore, there should be complexity in texture and image; the art should be representational and of high craft skill to be appreciated by the public. To discourage vandalism and graffiti it should be uncontroversial and non-political, it should avoid images which encourage doodles, e.g. speech bubbles or obscene appendages, and the surface should be modelled to provide a poor surface for graffiti and fly-posting.

23.8a (above) 'THE GRAPE PICKERS' BY RAYMOND MASON: bas-relief mural of form suitable for pedestrians.

23.8b (left) TBILISI, Georgia: excellent bas-relief, but political subjects should be avoided.

23.10a (below) GRAFFITI MURAL, Spain: 'Wild, wild and more wild'; Darren Ground – high artistic quality but prone to graffiti vandalism.

23.10b (right) GRAFFITI MURAL, Chur Station, Switzerland: excellent design but unsuitable for highway structures.

23.11a (left) PONT NOTRE-DAME, Paris. The keystone sculpture is integral to the bridge design.

23.11b (below) SCULPTED ELEPHANT KEYSTONE, Amsterdam: good detail near the zoo.

23.9 The materials used should not damage the surface or the structure, and should have a life compatible with the latter's maintenance cycle. Deteriorating murals look worse than dirty concrete. Graffiti-resistant coatings are generally of little use, since they themselves disfigure the surface and cleaning leaves smears and residues, especially on rough surfaces. The new generation of wax-based sacrificial coatings have some promise.

23.10 Graffiti art encourages more graffiti, which is highly unlikely to contain any artistic content, and can only detract from whatever artistic intent may have been in the first graffiti mural. A police study has found that where there is a high-quality graffiti mural, other graffiti sprayers come along to autograph over it. Graffiti art, therefore, is not usually suitable for murals on walls, bridges and tunnels.

23.11 As a basic principle, any art incorporated into a structure should be considered from the start as an integral part of the design, not introduced as an afterthought. It should also be specific to its particular context, both in subject matter and shape.

23.12a (left) KEIZERGRACHT BRIDGE, Radhuistraat. Piet Kramer's many bridges in Amsterdam show the successful integration of art and engineering.

23.12b (below) FREMONT TROLL, Aurora Avenue Bridge, Seattle: note inclusion of real car in the troll's right hand.

23.12c (above) LUXMOORES BRIDGE, Eton, Berkshire: artist-designed bridge.

23.13b (above) BLACKFRIARS BRIDGE, London. The bird is sculpted to avoid trapping water.

23.13a (right) VAUXHALL BRIDGE RIVER WALL, London. Water flows down the sculpted lion's mane and drips off it.

23.12 There have been too few successful integrations of art with civil engineering structures this century, but artists are now becoming involved to add environmental gains.

23.13 Where sculpture is used, it should be detailed to ensure there are no pockets to trap water, which may cause frost damage, and the form of the sculpture should allow for adequate drips to avoid staining by water runoff. Ledges which might attract rubbish or roosting birds should be avoided. Where sculpture is used, the importance of having realistic images over abstract forms is particularly important.

23.14a (left) CERAMIC MURAL, Komsomolskaya Station, Moscow: quality of detail appropriate for murals.

23.14b (left) EXETER STATION PAINTED MURAL: good quality of detail.

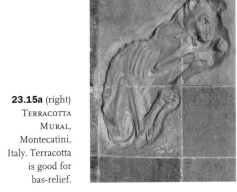

23.15a (right) TERRACOTTA MURAL, Montecatini, Italy. Terracotta is good for bas-relief.

23.16a (right) WILLEMSBRUG, Rotterdam. The bridge enhances the wire sculpture hanging across the foreground, but the sculpture is not beautiful in itself.

23.14 For murals near schools, the designs are often generated by competitions for local schoolchildren. This has the advantage that the children are less likely to deface their own work with graffiti. The translation into suitable materials and integration with the surface and form of the structure should be carried out professionally. The best artwork, whether murals or sculpture, is produced by talented professional artists, and such people should be commissioned wherever artwork is required.

23.15 Suitable materials for murals are ceramic tiles, mosaic, paint, brick, stone, laminate panels and enamel panels; for sculpture they are precast concrete, terracotta, ceramics, cast iron, bronze, stone and brick. Materials should be chosen for resistance to damage by vandals and long life with minimal maintenance, as well as appearance.

23.16 *All artwork used on bridges, tunnels and walls should be beautiful.*

Chapter 24
Signs and bridge furniture

INTRODUCTION

24.1 The appearance of a bridge is diminished through clutter and the incorporation of 'add on' bits such as lighting, signs, railings and barriers, whether on the bridge itself or part of the background setting of the structure. *As a first principle, it is therefore important to minimize clutter, not only on the bridge but also nearby.* The road corridor is often visually complex and the road user, as driver, passenger or pedestrian, is constantly confronted with visual information. The accumulation of signs and gantries, lighting, railings and masts make a functional and 'safe' environment but, at the same time, can cause visual chaos, disorder and intrusion, both in and outside the highway corridor.

24.2 Visual clarity of the structure with all its elements is essentially what the design team should be aiming for. Where essential street furniture such as railings or environmental barriers (see Highways Agency *Design Guide for Environmental Barriers HA 65/94*) are required, these should form part of the integrated design of the bridge, so that its appearance is not compromised and the whole structure creates the desired visual statement within the given landscape or townscape context.

24.3 This integration of a bridge with road furniture should take account of the historical and current landscape context, and should avoid undermining the local character and quality. Though this does not mean that radical and innovative design should be curbed, the design and integration of all the elements should recognize the significance and quality of the surrounding landscape in the choice of materials and the design as a whole – which might well, in some cases, mean

24.1a (above) M5/A38 INTERCHANGE, Lydiate Ash, Hereford & Worcester: direction signs crudely mounted on bridge superstructure.

24.1b (above, right) FOCKBURY MILL LANE BRIDGE, M5/M42 Interchange, Hereford & Worcester: ugly gantry too close to bridge.

24.1c (above) THE CITY, London. Cluttered accumulation of signs contributes to confusion and visual chaos.

24.2a (above, left) E40 MOTORWAY, Calais-Dunkirk, France: no clutter of signs.

24.3a (left) WEESP, Holland: a barrier appropriate to the surroundings, using various barrier types – transparent, sound-absorptive concrete, and planted.

24.10a (left) M6, Staffordshire. Planting helps to integrate signage into the landscape and screen it from outside views.

24.10b (below, left) M6, Staffordshire. Signs are often viewed against the sky. Planting would help to soften the stark silhouette.

24.10c (below) M3, Hampshire. Consideration should be given to the appearance and colouration of the reverse side of signs.

providing an interesting contrast. Roadside features such as planting, sculpture and street furniture may help to enliven a space and create an identity.

24.4 The colour of elements is an important factor, which requires attention as this can have a great influence on their integration into the landscape (see Chapter 21). The entire item should generally be one colour. Lanterns on top of lighting columns should usually be light in colour, unless they will be viewed against a dark background, or are designed to be a feature, as in a historic urban area. White, however, should be avoided, as it shows up against sky.

SIGNS

24.5 Signs, signage poles and support structures like gantries should, if possible, be kept off bridges and away from the 'visual envelope' or bridge setting. There is no point in designing a visually pleasing bridge only to find that large signs are to be placed on its façades, or even on gantries some metres away. It is therefore essential that bridge designers liaise closely with the signage and lighting designers to determine the best compromise possible (see also Chapter 2).

24.6 It must be possible in most cases to confine signs to the bridge approaches or, better still, before even the approaches are reached. On a large bridge, where signs may

have to be included because of its length or because instructions need to be displayed, they should be as discreet as possible, and preferably incorporated into the bridge structure on pylon bracing or girder bracing.

24.7 In general terms, signs should appear simple and elegant. Simple lines, no steps in section, constant cross-sectional shape, minimum number of different angles, and vertical main elements all help to simplify and clarify forms and make them less obtrusive, especially when seen against the vertical elements of buildings and trees.

24.8 Signs are often the only visual clue to the location of a road in a rural landscape, and care should be taken when designing the landscape and the mitigation proposals to help screen the signs as far as possible from the surroundings. The siting of these is governed by standards, but within the standard there is flexibility which should be fully exploited.

24.9 Generally most large signs look better when located as single elements in the landscape, and smaller signs appear better when grouped together in an ordered fashion.

24.10 Signs are less intrusive against a backdrop of hillside, woodland or vegetation. Planting behind a sign helps to break up its stark silhouette and softens the impact, but must be integrated into the overall landscape design. The colour of the rear of signs also needs to be taken into account, and the possible integration may well be enhanced by a colour study of the dominant background against which the sign would be viewed. The back and the supports could then be painted a suitable hue to blend in better with the surroundings.

24.13a (far left) M3, Surrey. Contemporary technology still needs to be integrated into the landscape.

24.13b (left) M25. Gantries and signs can have a severe impact outside the highway corridor.

24.13c (right) M3, Surrey. Excessive mass and form of gantries and signs have a significant impact within the highway corridor.

24.13d (below) Motorway, Holland. Lightweight and light-coloured gantries appear less intrusive in the landscape.

24.13e (below) Motorway, Belgium. Lightweight lattice structure is appropriately sized to support variable message sign.

24.11 Reduction in weight of signs also reduces the need for massive support structures. This means that signs should be designed to an optimum without any redundant spaces or superfluous materials. As materials technology improves, the weight of signs may decrease, which will further reduce the mass of their supports.

24.12 Illumination of signs should avoid the creation of upwards light spillage, which causes light pollution (see Fig. 28.10a).

GANTRIES

24.13 Gantries spanning motorway and trunk road carriageways are generally large steel structures, visually apparent for long distances within the motorway corridor, and often seen from areas outside it as well. Gantries must fail safely if hit by a vehicle. This means they must either stay in position with no parts falling off onto the carriageway, or they must fail so that they collapse off the carriageway. The former is the approach generally taken to date in the UK. This means that the gantry and its supports are robust elements,

generally out of character with the surroundings. The latter approach gives a visually lighter structure and is common in the rest of Europe. Maintenance requiring access over the highway on the gantry has certain safety requirements which pose restrictions on the form, mass and appearance.

24.14 It may be possible to protect the support structures of the gantries or to remove them from the immediate edge of the road corridor, thereby reducing the risk of impact and possible collapse, as well as the size of the supports, which would no longer have to withstand such collisions.

COLUMNS AND MASTS

24.15 Apart from lighting columns and sign poles, a number of columns or masts relate to traffic management, carrying CCTV cameras, traffic speeding cameras and radio transmitters. These add to the visual clutter alongside roads. The function of the cameras dictates to a large degree where the apparatus may be placed, but consideration must also be given to the relation of these features to signs and other landscape features within and outside the road corridor.

Speed cameras tend to be needed where the speed limit does not agree with the perceived speed of the road. Increasing the speed limit by removing dangerous features such as awkward junctions removes the need for clutter and can improve pollution, safety and traffic flow.

24.16 Some of these different types of apparatus are located on high masts visible well outside the road corridor. All such equipment should preferably be placed on columns already needed for other purposes, or on adjacent buildings; but where this is not possible the masts and apparatus should be placed away from other items such as lighting columns and signs so as to decongest the visual core of the road corridor. The colour of the columns should be treated in a similar way to all columns.

PARAPETS AND GUARDS

24.17 Parapets are an important feature on any bridge. Although DoT design standards on safety principles should normally be adhered to, where possible all parapets and railings should complement the bridge's structure and may even be used as a significant and decisive element of its design. Railing depth, shape and spacings between horizontal members and vertical supports are key issues.

Due consideration must also be given to solid parapets where the introduction of pattern and texture may add interest to pedestrians. Colour is also a key consideration; it can help to give a bridge or series of bridges, as along a stretch of motorway, a particular identity. Drivers who use the routes often would also be able to identify the bridge and their location along the route.

Timber parapets look particularly good on timber bridges, weathering steel bridges and in many rustic situations, particularly footbridges.

24.18 High, solid parapet screens, as for equestrian bridges, should be avoided as they appear massive in relation to the bridge supports and deck structure. If possible, mesh screens, which appear solid when viewed obliquely from above by the horse and rider, should be used. These appear less solid and massive when approached face on. The bottom parts of these panels may have to be solid. The colour of such panels and mesh should be related to the surrounding landscape and the most frequent viewing locations (see Paragraph 21.4).

Equestrian parapets are very ugly and out of scale generally, and are very unpleasant for pedestrians, especially on a narrow bridge. They should not be provided where there is vehicular use of the bridge, since horses are required to use the road, to protect pedestrians, and are then separated from the parapet by the verge or footpath. Mounting blocks can be provided to avoid the need for equestrian parapets, but these should be located such that horses are not disturbed by the traffic during dismounting. Heavy equestrian usage, e.g. near a riding school, will often make equestrian parapets necessary on road bridges.

24.17a (top) E40 MOTORWAY, Calais-Dunkirk. Bold use of colour, plus distinctive pier forms, add visual interest for drivers.

24.17b (above) A18 MOTORWAY, Belgium. Distinct use of colour helps driver orientation.

24.18a (right) EQUESTRIAN SCREEN. The necessary height makes an unattractive corridor for pedestrians.

SAFETY FENCING (CRASH BARRIERS)

24.19 It is often quite difficult to integrate safety barriers into the overall scheme. However, due consideration must be given to these articles in the design of the bridge, and where possible they should be placed unobtrusively. There are many types of safety fencing currently in use, and some of the less common types can have visual advantages. The corrugated and box beam barriers appear more solid than the cable type. Care must be taken in choosing these barriers as their appearance is different and they may influence the overall appearance of the bridge. On no account should safety fences be painted, unless there is the commitment to maintain the painted surface for the life of the bridge. Safety fences which have been painted and have received no maintenance appear shoddy and diminish the quality of the local surroundings. The use of safety barriers between the road and pedestrians can permit the use of non-standard bridge parapets without the need for expensive destructive testing, as also can high kerbs on low-speed, narrow roads.

RAILINGS, FENCES AND STREET FURNITURE

24.20 Generic, stock solutions are used all too often for these features, whereas a total design concept would help to create a much more pleasant and aesthetic appearance. Their colour also needs to be considered, as well as their co-ordination with the colour, texture and pattern of other landscape elements such as paved surfaces and planting. Bollards, seating, lighting, bus shelters, bins, planters, etc. all help to create a lasting image that can improve as well as detract from a particular landscape/townscape setting. Furthermore, a well co-ordinated scheme will reduce clutter and enhance mobility through a space as well as providing a particular appearance and identity for each individual location. In rural areas fences should be kept below the skylines, especially on cuttings. Fences, hedges and walls should repeat vernacular forms and traditional geometry related to topography for their positions (see Paragraph 29.16).

24.19a (left) HOLLAND: corrugated beam barrier well integrated with girder structure of bridge.

24.20a (below) A4, Hammersmith. A sympathetic treatment of pedestrian railings which does not diminish landscape quality. Planting helps to improve appearance.

24.19b (left) PARIS: separate crash and transparent acoustic barriers.

24.21a (left) Périphérique, Paris: luxuriant vegetation on the bridge itself.

24.21c (below) La Défense, Paris. Hedge on footbridge acts as a windbreak.

Planters

24.21 One does not often see planters used on bridges. However, in certain instances, like areas surrounded by woodland or other vegetation, the introduction of planting onto a bridge structure can help to integrate it into the landscape setting and may well provide a pleasant approach for pedestrians and motorists using the bridge. This is valid also in urban areas, where the visual shortening of a bridge by continued avenue planting or other more formal streetscape can reduce the severance effect of a new road in cutting through to an urban area (see Fig. 29.31a).

Great care has to be taken to design these planters in scale with the bridge and to ensure that they are able to sustain adequate and healthy plant growth. The type of plant material, depth of planter, soil characteristics, irrigation and maintenance requirements should all be assessed by a landscape architect.

24.21b (above, left) Périphérique, Pantin, Paris. Planting on the embankment both screens traffic and links the bridge visually with the surrounding landscape.

24.22a (above) Motorway, Holland. Advertising appears incongruous within rural areas.

Hoardings and Other Signs

24.22 Advertising hoardings close to the road corridor intrude on the landscape, although they may appear as focal points of interest from the road corridor. The incorporation of advertising adjacent to roads in urban areas is generally an accepted form of communication, which has the ability, depending on the quality of the message, as well as the structure it appears on, to enhance or diminish townscape quality. Advertising in rural/semi-rural areas generally appears incongruous and out of place. Where signs are used, as in much of the rest of Europe, to promote the facilities of a town or village which is bypassed, the character of the sign can benefit from appearing different and less formal than other official signs. The clarity of the message should not, however, be reduced.

24.23 One type of sign not often used in the UK, but common in other European countries, is that which names the bridge (see Fig. 20.36a). This sign may be an important feature. Where bridges cross streams, rivers, railway lines, local features or roads they could be named and signed. To do so sets the structure within its local and national context. Names also help to identify locations for travellers and the emergency services. The naming of any structure should be subject to discussions with national and local interest groups and be agreed with the relevant authorities. Bridge numbering should, however, be placed discreetly.

Picture Credits
24.21c ph JW. All other photographs by Arup.

Chapter 25
Bridges adjacent to existing bridges

25.1 Where a new bridge has to be built close to an existing one, it is important that it should not be too near. *The main reason for preserving an existing bridge without alteration when it is structurally inadequate or too small for future use is to enable people to enjoy the view of it in its setting. If a new bridge is built immediately alongside, this enjoyment is lost, certainly as seen from one side and quite possibly from both. It is usually well worthwhile keeping a reasonable distance away and diverting the approaches as may be necessary.*

25.2 *When a new bridge is built near an existing bridge purely for increase in capacity, as with motorway widening, unless the bridges are identical it is best to space them sufficiently apart to appreciate the view of each where possible (see also Chapter 11).*

25.3 If the two bridges must be close to one another, there is generally an aesthetic advantage in making them parallel, and with the same vertical profile.

25.4 In the design of a new bridge to be erected near an old one, it is usually a mistake to copy the old work, though an exception might be where an existing bridge of fairly conventional design, say a small 18th-century bridge in an urban setting, is to be duplicated for one-way traffic.

25.5 Normally the new bridge should be a good example of its own period, acting perhaps as a foil or contrast to the old bridge, whether or not similar materials are used. The contrast between old work of massive construction and new work of concrete or steel can often be exploited effectively; this contrast, however, should not be to the detriment of the immediate area.

25.3a (top) TAMAR BRIDGES, Saltash, Cornwall: same vertical profile.

25.4a (above) BERWICK BRIDGES, Northumberland. There is no need to copy earlier bridges.

25.5c (above, right) A69 LANERCOST BRIDGES, Cumbria: contrast of heavy and light construction.

25.5a (above) PILAR BRIDGE, Zaragoza, Spain: contrast of traditional and modern design.

25.1a (top) PILGRIM'S WAY BRIDGE, Guildford: the new bridge gives space to see the Lutyens bridge.

25.5b (left) ELVET BRIDGES, Durham.

25.6a (below) GIGGLESWICK BRIDGE, North Yorkshire.

25.6b (left) KINGSFERRY BRIDGE, Isle of Sheppey, Kent: proposed high-level arch bridge adjacent to existing lifting bridge.

25.7a (above) BOCKING BRIDGES, Essex.

25.6 The problem is different in the case of a new bridge dominating its older neighbour by sheer size, or that of a light footbridge forming little more than an appendage to an existing bridge. In the former case, keeping a reasonable distance becomes the more important factor; although relative levels may sometimes require equal consideration, it is best for levels to be either identical or dramatically different. In the latter case, while distance is still important, the detailed design and the element of contrast are what matter most.

25.7 The use of timber pedestrian bridges as suitable accompaniments to ancient stone bridges, to which timber seems a natural foil, is often a very successful solution.

25.8 It is very important to ensure that the full opening size and shape of any existing bridge is not visually blocked by a new bridge when viewed both through the old bridge and through the new, and from all major viewpoints. When the old

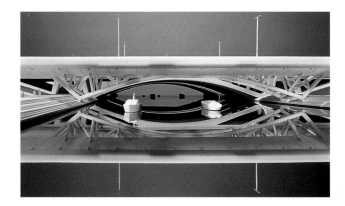

25.8a (left) RUNNYMEDE, River
Thames: proposal for new bridge.

25.12a (below) WENTBRIDGE,
Yorkshire: proposed alignments.

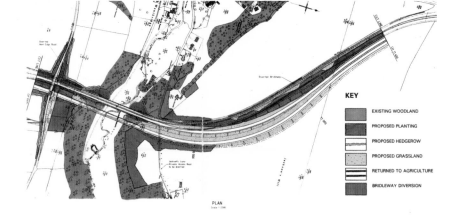

25.11a (below) MEDWAY BRIDGES,
Kent: relationship of two new
crossings to the existing.

25.11b (bottom) MESOCCO
BRIDGE, Switzerland. Offset piers
can aid transparency.

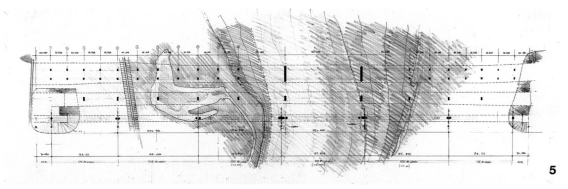

5

bridge has a dominant-shaped opening such as a major arch, the new bridge should preferably repeat this shape. This does not mean that the structural form needs to be copied. For instance, at Runnymede a masonry arch form is repeated in concrete and as a three-dimensioned steel truss. The only exception to this is when an existing ugly or unsympathetic bridge is to be masked by a more beautiful or environmentally sympathetic structure.

25.9 When the opening shape is not repeated, the opening shape of the new bridge should be sympathetic to the old, and their visual relationship taken into account.

25.10 It is often attractive as well as structurally appropriate for new structures to be more visually light and delicate than adjacent older structures. Where this cannot be the case, such as with stouter columns and deeper beams for changed regulations on basically similar structures, as in motorway widening, there is an argument for increasing spans or reducing column numbers to visually make the extra member size seem logical. It is not recommended to fatten up the existing to match the new.

25.11 New piers should generally be aligned with existing piers, but this does not mean that every old pier should have a new pier to match. In exceptional situations, where views of the two structures are restricted, the piers can be positioned out of orthogonal alignment to give greater

25.14a (right) Runnymede
Bridge, River Thames:
catenary lighting.

25.12b (below) Wentbridge
Yorkshire. Different coloured
foliage of non-native trees
emphasizes large abutment
built out from valley side.

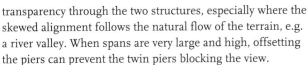

transparency through the two structures, especially where the
skewed alignment follows the natural flow of the terrain, e.g.
a river valley. When spans are very large and high, offsetting
the piers can prevent the twin piers blocking the view.

25.12 The shape, position and size of abutments – whether
concrete, masonry or earth bunds – should be carefully
integrated and modelled into their immediate context. Careful
co-ordination between the engineer, architect and landscape
architect is vital. Bridges of the 1950s and 1960s tended to
have large earth bunds projecting into valleys to shorten
spans. Modern structures should span right across the valley
without intrusive bunds, therefore the integration of such new
and old abutments needs to be carefully handled, especially
where it is possible (it is always desirable) to retain existing
mature planting.

25.13 When bridges cross rivers, with piers in the river,
there is often a need to provide additional protection
from scour and from collision by ships and boats – either
because of current, more onerous requirements or because the
new bridge is likely to cause changes to the water flow which
might increase the scour or collision danger. Artificial islands
of rocks or piled structure are often used (see Chapter 14), but
their use must be carried out with great caution, particularly
on tidal rivers where they can stand up to 10m above water

level. The elegance of a new or older structure can be ruined
by 'gumboots on a ballerina'. A joint island for a new and old
structure is almost always to be avoided, since the size and
scale are even more excessive, and the two structures tend to
lose their clarity and separate identity. Any islands should
strive towards naturalness.

25.14 Lighting columns on bridges are always a difficult
element to handle well (see Chapter 22), but cause
particular problems where two bridges are immediately
adjacent, since lighting columns aligning with piers and
structural bays of one bridge may then not align with the
other. Lighting should be avoided and/or lamp columns
minimized. Catenary lighting can minimize columns.
Lighting columns placed in between the two bridges to light
both roads can be a good solution, since they are then the
maximum distance from an observer, and parallax can obscure
misalignment of the structural bays. Where a major new
bridge is adjacent to a minor old bridge, the structures are
best lit separately.

PICTURE CREDITS
25.1a d Arup. **25.3a** ph JW. **25.4a** ph Collections. **25.5a d** Cevezo, Julvez
y Ocezo; ph OP. **25.5b** ph JW. **25.6b d** Arup; illus. Fred English. **25.7a**
ph JW. **25.8a d** Ahrends Burton & Koralek. **25.11a d** Percy Thomas
Partnership. **25.11b d** Christian Menn; ph JW. **25.12b d** Yorkshire
County Council; ph JW. **25.14a d** Arup; ph JW.

Chapter 26

Bridge widening, alteration and reuse

WIDENING

26.1 Road widening, and in particular motorway widening, has recently been seen as a more environmentally friendly way of accommodating increased road traffic, in that it utilizes the existing road corridor rather than creating a new transport corridor. This has led to the need to widen (or, more accurately, broaden) many relatively recent underbridges (for overbridges, see Chapter 19). This can be done in three ways:
- building a new bridge near to the existing (see Chapter 25)
- replacing the existing (see Chapter 11)
- extending the breadth of the existing on either or both sides.
In all cases, the widened bridge should look as though it was always intended to be like that: a unity between new and old.

26.2 *When a bridge is broadened, the opportunity should be taken to improve on the existing design where it does not correspond with the advice in this publication, and is not beautiful.* This is in accordance with the policy of improving landscaping and environmental amelioration when motorways are widened.

26.3 Where a bridge is broadened only on one side, the advice above should be followed for that side where it is a small structure and both faces are not seen as an entity. On larger bridges, the structure is usually read more as a three-dimensional object, and so the façades should not read significantly differently.

26.4 *Rebuilding an identical façade or structure is often the simplest and ultimately the least controversial solution,* despite being the most obvious. Where the original structure had relatively elegant or sophisticated details, these should

generally be repeated accurately; a crude simplification of details is almost never visually successful.

26.5 Culverts should be lengthened with the same cross-section, but not necessarily the same form of construction. Any new portal should follow the advice in Chapter 18. It is unlikely to be necessary to match the existing portal.

26.6 Pedestrian and equestrian underpasses should follow the advice in Chapter 16. Since the portals and their approaches are among the most critical elements of the design, pedestrian underpasses have particular scope for improvement when the road is widened, especially since the lengthened underpass would otherwise be significantly less satisfactory than the existing.

26.7 Small single-span underbridges should continue the same cross-section when the breadth will exceed the span in the widened structure. This is particularly important in bridges over canals and navigable rivers, where there should be no physical or visual pinch points.

26.8 Multi-span bridges should follow the advice above, but they have further complexities. Pier or column positions should be located so that they align with the existing. Leaf piers should either be extended to match the existing in all details, or if the bridge is broadened symmetrically, piers or columns can be added in line, with their details similar. On small structures it is rarely successful to change the shape of columns or change alignment from the existing, since the widening will generally be subservient to the existing, especially if the widening is asymmetrical. Similarly, abutments should be treated in a similar way to the existing and on the same alignment. Cantilevering the new structure off the old is frequently best in that it avoids all changes to substructure and usually improves the section proportions by making the deck appear more slender. If needed, cantilever brackets should align with existing structural bays or modules of balustrades, etc. Cantilever brackets can add to the visual interest, helping to reduce the bridge's scale, but the simplicity

26.4a (above) M40 BRIDGE, River Avon, Warwick Bypass, Warwickshire: façade rebuilt further over – the least controversial solution.

26.9a (above) AVON BRIDGE, Royal Leamington Spa, Warwickshire: widening for pedestrians. The spindly columns almost look like rainwater pipes.

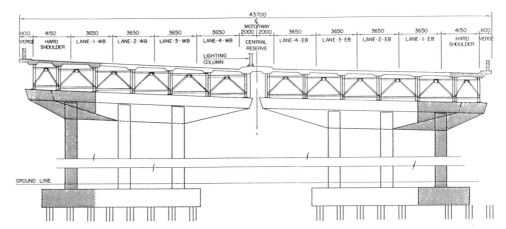

26.9b (right) M40 Bridge, High Wycombe, Buckinghamshire: widened by repeating cantilever and column.

26.10a (below) Rodenkirchen Suspension Bridge, Germany: widened by adding new cable.

26.10b (left) George Washington Bridge, New York: second deck added beneath the first.

of a cantilever slab with no brackets should be exploited where possible.

Broadening a bridge will make the land under end-spans less viable for plants since it will be drier and darker. The treatment should be co-ordinated with the landscape architect and the advice in Chapter 28 followed.

26.9 A particular problem with large multi-span bridges and viaducts is that the additional road width can be proportionally minor compared with the existing – too great for a cantilever, yet too small for an addition column on the same module as the existing. This can be overcome by widening asymmetrically to give enough structure for an additional full bay in some situations. Placing the vehicle barrier between the road and the pedestrians can enable the pedestrian deck to have lighter loadings; this can then be a lighter structure on a cantilever. Alternatively, the pedestrian route can be separated onto either a completely separate structure well clear of the existing bridge or, perhaps, incorporated below the deck. Another solution is to widen the outermost columns into a short leaf pier, possibly with an integral cantilever at the head to support the extra strip of deck. This works best if it is symmetrical on both sides of the bridge. On relatively low bridges where there is already a clutter of columns, it may be an improvement to block off open end-bays with walls, thus hiding a worsening clutter of structure. The treatment of these walls must be handled very sensitively and considered as part of the overall appearance of the bridge. This approach may be more appropriate in urban areas where the space under the end-spans might otherwise cause a vandalism problem, and there are no views of

landscape flowing through the bridge. A narrow strip of deck supported on spindly columns as an extension to a structure which is broad and supported on proportionally massive columns should be avoided.

26.10 Major estuarial crossings and other structures with single spans over 150m must be considered on a one-off basis. It is more usual to have a separate structure alongside to accommodate additional traffic. However, other techniques have been successful:
● adding an additional deck above or below the existing
● adding a third cable to a suspension bridge
● infilling between twin structures.

All the previous advice in this chapter may be valid for the approach spans.

26.11 When widening bridges over canals and rivers, moving the banks or navigable channel should be avoided if possible, but where unavoidable the banks should look natural on a river, and should avoid sharp corners, chicanes, etc., on canals. Any additional bank protection should be anticipated at the outset and designed carefully into the scheme.

ALTERATIONS TO HISTORIC BRIDGES

26.12 When works to a historic bridge are proposed, even where only some of it is extant, the historic parts should be considered of primary importance in the new design and conserved, unless proved beyond doubt to be unviable.

Early concrete and steel bridges can be of just as much concern as Roman, medieval or classical bridges.

When works are proposed to any historic bridge, the full history of the site and structures should be studied by suitably experienced archaeologists and/or industrial archaeologists, both on site and through archives. This should include information on both the original form, dates, designers and materials, and on any subsequent major alterations, and graphic recording of what is still extant from the various dates. Note should also be made of any historic associations, such as reference by painters, poets, etc.

This information should form part of the basic brief to the engineer and architect.

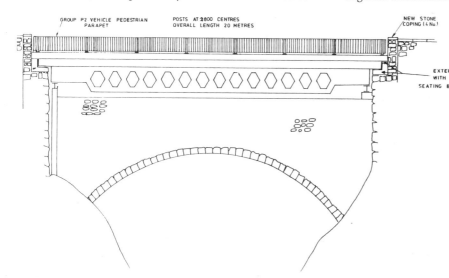

26.12a (left) DEVIL'S BRIDGE, Dyfed, Wales: how not to alter a historic bridge.

26.12c (below) M1 BRIDGE: some of the first motorway bridges in Britain, now considered for listing.

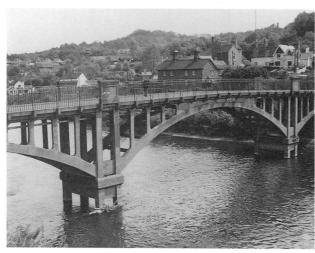

26.12b (above) FREEBRIDGE, Ironbridge Gorge, Shropshire: an important early reinforced concrete bridge.

26.12d (right) PONT DU GARD, Nimes, France. The first tier of this Roman aqueduct was doubled in width to the identical arch profile in the 18th century.

26.12e (left) PONT NEUF, Paris. Replacement of old stone, and especially carving, should be avoided unless it is actually unsafe.

26.12f (below) CLOPTON BRIDGE, Stratford-upon-Avon. 18th-century stone widening and 19th-century cast iron widening are of as much historical interest as the medieval bridge.

26.15a (left) RENNIE'S LONDON BRIDGE: cantilever widening removed on remaining arch.

26.13a (above) AULD BRIG, Stirling, Central Region, Scotland: old bridge retained and restored after bypassing.

26.15b (right) BEDFORD TOWN BRIDGE: 1960s lighting removed.

26.13 An old bridge may be of such outstanding importance as a historical monument that neither its demolition nor any alteration to its appearance should be accepted. The difficulties may be overcome by constructing a bypass, and it should be emphasized that where this is contemplated, every effort should be made to avoid disturbing the old bridge. In other cases it may be necessary to build a new bridge alongside (see Fig. 25.5a). The existing bridge may still have to be repaired and can be used as a footbridge.

26.14 The structure may have been scheduled as an Ancient Monument or listed as of special architectural or historical interest or be in a conservation area, in which case the relevant authorities should be consulted. Many bridges not so listed may also be of such intrinsic interest that a strong case could be established for their preservation.

26.15 *In those cases where it is accepted that an old bridge may be altered, it may still be important to ensure that such alterations are carried out with minimum change in outward appearance. Such changes should generally aim for simplicity rather than elaboration, and also tend towards restoring features lost in previous alterations, where there is clear evidence of what existed previously. Any replica parts should be in the proper material.*

26.16 If the existing bridge is merely narrow rather than structurally weak, it may be possible to use it, with or without strengthening, as a one-way bridge. In such a case, it may be necessary to build another bridge alongside or nearby. Again, the width of the bridge may be adequate for two-way traffic if existing pedestrian traffic is eliminated, and for this purpose a pedestrian footbridge alongside or nearby may be all that is required.

26.17 Where widening is necessary, it is sometimes assumed that, provided the elevational treatment is kept the same, nothing else matters. This is not necessarily so. The pictorial effect of an old bridge may well depend upon its width seen through an arch, the amount of sky visible obliquely, or the amount of scenery visible below the sky. It is usually best to widen on only one side.

26.18 For the above reason, in the past it was often considered better aesthetically to keep the existing arch or arches as they were and cantilever out for additional width. This approach, however, is only rarely successful and requires the utmost care and attention to detail to succeed.

26.16a (below) BROCKHAM BRIDGE, Surrey: pedestrian bridge built alongside to give extra vehicle width.

26.16b (below, right) SKIRLAW BRIDGE, Bishop Auckland, Co. Durham: one-way traffic and a cantilevered pedestrian walkway.

26.16c (right) LOSTWITHIEL BRIDGE, Cornwall. The sign itself is of historical interest.

26.18b (below) ALDEA DEL FRESNO BRIDGE, Madrid, Spain. Simple and effective cantilever widening, though some of the rustic quality is still lost.

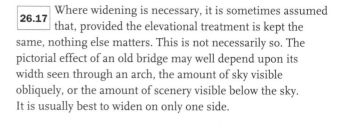

26.18a (above) ALGETE BRIDGE, Madrid, Spain: successful cantilever widening.

26.18c (left) WILTON BRIDGE, Ross-on-Wye, Hereford & Worcester. Crude details help to spoil this bridge.

26.19a (above) Bridgnorth Bridge, Shropshire: dominance of piers kept in widening.

26.19b (left) Aixe-sur-Vienne, Périgord, France. Dominance of cutwaters is retained.

26.19c (above) Wilton Bridge, Ross-on-Wye. Crude widening has destroyed the charm of the bridge. The 14th-century obelisk and sundial also went.

26.19 With heavier medieval bridges, in which the cutwaters are carried up between the arches to form embrasures in a continuous solid parapet, widening the whole structure and refacing may be the better answer. Where the embrasures are sufficiently large to not be lost by widening, beams spanning between them can be successful. Where the widening is sited on the cutwaters, and their heavy, vertical, punctuating emphasis is replaced by a relatively light, filigree, horizontal feel, this is at odds with the structural form.

26.19d (above, centre) Wilton Bridge, Ross-on-Wye. The unwidened side is still beautiful.

26.19e (above) Brecon Bridge, Powys, Wales. Dominance of cutwater is lost.

26.20a (below) Pont d'Iena, Paris: widened by rebuilding façade on extension.

26.21b (below, centre) Verde Bridge, Granada, Spain: ends of parapet also cantilevered in widening.

26.21a (below) Talamanca de Jarama Bridge, Madrid, Spain: successful treatment of parapet over cantilever.

26.21c (left) Brecon Bridge, Powys, Wales: crude treatment of soffit.

26.21e (bottom, left) Pont Des Invalides, Paris. Cantilevered edge-widening slabs continue dentil course and tie in well with abutment pier.

26.21d (above) Helland Bridge, Cornwall: masonry parapet cantilevered on corbels – an excellent traditional detail.

26.20 With the lighter classical type of bridge, the extra width can be provided by a cantilever slab or a slab on a series of brackets. However, again *refacing the bridge to match the existing may be the best solution, especially now that there has been a revival in the skills of traditional and classical design and in the necessary quality of craftsmanship.*

The satisfactory design and placing of these brackets raises problems of exceptional difficulty from the point of view of finished appearance. The situation varies so much with different bridges that no general principle can be laid down, but the aim should be to maintain as far as possible the logic that lies at the root of classical design. If, for example, there is a full entablature above the arch, the transverse brackets should be inserted in the frieze if possible, the architrave being left intact and the cornice reproduced on the new outer edge.

26.21 The treatment of the parapet over the cantilevered portion is another difficulty. A classical stone balustrade, for example, that looks satisfactory in the plane of the spandrels may well look too heavy if brought forward and carried on brackets, as well as being structurally undesirable.

Special consideration must be given to the ends of the parapet in this sort of cantilevered widening. Very often the ends of the original bridge will have been curved round to form a smooth junction with the embankment on either side, or possibly a reverse quadrant will have been inserted between the two to punctuate the transition. All of this should be cantilevered. The appearance from a pedestrian's point of view when crossing the bridge is very important, especially the relationship to bridgehead buildings. In all cases the detailed design of the widening, especially as seen from below, calls for very careful study if the effect is not to appear makeshift. A masonry parapet is best when a masonry arch is used instead of a cantilever.

26.22 Mention may be made here of alterations to bridge approaches. Whether an existing approach is to be widened on one or both sides, or whether it is to be supplemented by a separate approach to the new bridge, special attention should be paid to the treatment of any new embankments and retaining walls, to the layout and treatment of any small open space, whether paved or planted, between

the old and new work, and to the connection between the parapet of the bridge and that of the embankment. Even if the new work is designed to contrast to some extent with the old, a proper junction between the two is essential. Careful consideration for the retention of existing trees and bridgehead buildings is very important to enhance the setting of the new and old bridges.

26.23 It is often assumed that existing parapets have to be replaced, but the greatest effort should be made to avoid this, unless the existing parapet is already an inappropriate replacement. A separate vehicle barrier between the road and the pavement is often a good solution, although it has disadvantages with regard to streetscape. It should be as simple and as low as possible.

26.24 A plaque recording the building and restoration of historic bridges is often called for. This is appropriate but should be built into the bridge, not stuck on as an afterthought (see Chapters 3 and 23).

26.21f (above) LEITH BRIDGE, Leith, Edinburgh: concrete cantilever textured and old stone parapet reused.

26.22a (right) BOSTON BRIDGE, Lincolnshire. Relationship to bridgehead buildings is important.

26.21g (top) MONMOUTH BRIDGE, Wales: widened by additional shallow stone arch springing between old cutwaters, saving ornamental pinnacles and reusing stone parapet.

26.23a (above) OLD LANDQUART BRIDGE, Klosters, Switzerland: parapet reinforced with concrete barrier.

26.24a (right) BROCKHAM BRIDGE, Surrey: plaque.

REUSING EXISTING BRIDGES

26.25 When the opportunity occurs, the possibility of reusing existing structures for new roads should always be examined. Redundant railway viaducts and bridges provide an environmentally advantageous solution for new roads, especially in environmentally sensitive areas. Restoring and converting historic structures can positively benefit a road scheme.

26.26 The conversion may be low-key and unobtrusive (see Fig. 15.2d) but more often, substantial change is required. Research should be carried out to ensure that nothing of historic value is unnecessarily lost, and that anything which has to be lost is at least recorded.

26.27 In principle, any element which is new should be expressed as something contemporary (though in harmony with the old), but any retained element should be carefully restored. Where an element must be changed, a pastiche of a historical style is rarely the right approach.

26.28 To judge whether an item to be amended is an element in itself, so should be contemporary, or is only part of an element, and therefore should be restored, is difficult and the advice of an architect experienced in conservation work may be useful on such schemes. The advice of the Society for the Protection for Ancient Buildings (SPAB) is also useful.

26.29 An element should be complete and consistent in itself so that, for instance, where new piers or the extension of piers are required, the new work should match the old. If a new arch of similar size is required, if certain members of a truss are to be replaced, if brickwork or stonework is to be patched, all should match the existing. If a few additional tie bars are required, the face plates should match the existing, even if they are not an original part of the structure. If new abutments are required at the ends of a viaduct, they should not be discordant elements which interrupt the flow of the existing structure. However, they may either match the existing or be a new element, such as a bankseat, depending on the particular situation.

26.26a (left) NEWBRIDGE ON WYE, Powys, Wales: new concrete arches on old stone piers of former bridge.

26.25a (below) NEWTON CAP VIADUCT, Durham: railway viaduct being converted to road bridge.

26.29a (left) BRAY VIADUCT, Devon: extended piers and new piers to match originals.

26.30a (left) Britannia Bridge, Menai Straits: new spans expressed on two-tier alteration after a fire.

26.30b (left) Waverley Bridge, Edinburgh: ugly plastic cladding panels imitating cast iron.

26.30d (above) Augustine Bridge, Wilmington, USA. Trussed structure echoes form of original bridge.

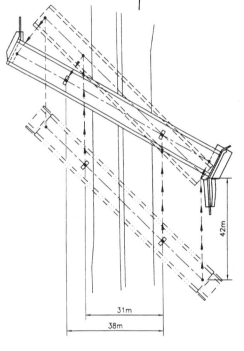

26.30c (right) Green Street/Green Overbridge, Dartford, Kent. Skew reduced to increase span from 31m to 38m – reused deck on new abutments.

26.30 Though a new element should be expressed as contemporary (Fig. 7.2e), the appearance of the total structure should be the principal consideration in its detailed design. Where a new enlarged span is required in a multi-span structure, or a replacement span is required between large architectural abutments, a contemporary form is probably best, but each case should be judged on its merits. It is important that the form of the total structure is considered when designing the new span. Also the quantity of detail should be similar to the existing spans and other parts to ensure that the scale and complexity of the existing structure is maintained. The replacement of riveted fabricated girders with welded flush smooth girders or box beams can cause particular problems with quantity of detail. A more visually complex form of structure should be chosen when extra detail is required, e.g. trusses, especially three-dimensional ones, and bolted connections. Applied decoration or false imitation of historic detailing are almost invariably wrong.

26.30e (above) Grand Avenue Bridge, Eau Claire, Wisconsin, USA. New deck is too small for old piers.

26.33a (left) Auld Brig, Stirling:
bridge well-restored for pedestrian use.

26.33b (left)
Windsor
Town Bridge,
Berkshire:
pedestrianized
and popular
with tourists.

26.33c (above) Puente Romano,
Granada, Spain: well-restored
4th-century Roman bridge,
recently pedestrianized.

26.31 When made redundant by a new bridge, the reuse of a historic bridge for pedestrians, etc., can be a positive environmental advantage to a scheme, but some work to make the old bridge suitable for its new use is usually required.

26.32 Sufficient space to see and appreciate the old bridge is required (see Chapter 25) and suitable approaches to the new use should be retained or formed. Redundant street furniture such as signs and road lighting should be removed. Where the route of the old road is still accessible and traffic needs to be excluded from the bridge, this is better done by using pedestrian finishes and suitable hard landscaping to discourage traffic, with bollards if necessary. Putting a fence across the road is rarely an appropriate solution.

26.33 Where the old bridge is of historic importance, a more thorough approach to conversion for pedestrian use should be made. The road surface should be removed and replaced with something more appropriate. If there are archive photographs, or physical evidence remains, these should be used as the basis for new paving and all restoration work. Where the old bridge has been widened by cantilevering a deck, by removing parapets or embrasures, or by adding a pedestrian footway to the edge, these preferably should be removed. Where parapets have been altered or removed, these should be restored to their original form, unless the current parapets themselves are of historic interest. Where bridgehead buildings have been removed in the past to improve approaches or sightlines, redevelopment of these sites to restore the townscape should be encouraged.

26.34 In an urban situation, floodlighting a particularly important bridge can be considered to enhance the environmental amelioration and deter graffiti. This is also valid for historic bridges retained in use, especially where they are being altered.

Picture Credits
26.4a ph JW. **26.9b d** Halcrow. **26.10a d** Rendel Palmer & Tritton. **26.10b d** OH Ammann; ph Robert Harding Picture Library. **26.12b d** François Hennebique. **26.12c d** Owen Williams. **26.12d** ph JW. **26.12e** ph JW. **26.12f** ph JW. **26.13a** ph JW. **26.15a d** John Rennie; ph JW. **26.15b** ph JW. **26.16a** ph JW. **26.16b** ph JW. **26.16c** ph JW. **26.18a d** Ordóñez y Calzón; ph Jafo. **26.18b d** Ordóñez y Calzón. **26.18c** ph JW. **26.19b d** Alain Spielmann. **26.19c** ph JW. **26.19d** ph JW. **26.19e** ph JW. **26.20a** ph JW. **26.21a d** Ordóñez y Calzón. **26.21b d** Ordóñez y Calzón. **26.21c** ph JW. **26.21d** ph JW. **26.21e** ph JW. **26.21f** ph JW. **26.23a** ph JW. **26.24a** ph JW. **26.25a d** Durham County Council/ Bullen. **26.29a d**/ph Gifford Graham. **26.30a d** Robert Stephenson; ph JW. **26.30b** ph JW. **26.30c d** Mott MacDonald. **26.30d d** Pavlo Engineering Co. **26.30e d** Owen Ayres Associates. **26.33a** ph JW. **26.33b d** Sir Jeffrey Wyatville; ph JW. **26.33c d** Ordóñez y Calzón.

Chapter 27

Use of space under bridges

27.1 There are two interrelated aspects of the use of space under bridges – function and finishes.

27.2 *The function of the space under bridges* – apart from the river, road or railway, etc., being crossed – *is most usually to continue the flow of the landscape through beneath the bridge.* This is specifically relevant to open-end spans associated with bankseats, and to viaducts. Materials appropriate to the visual continuation of soft landscaping under end-spans, etc., are covered below.

27.3 Where a viaduct passes over agricultural land, it is best visually to continue that use under the viaduct. Fencing off the land under a bridge or viaduct is unnecessary, visually obtrusive and should be avoided. Even where the land is poorer, due to the drier and more shaded conditions under the structure, it is generally better under agriculture since bare soil looks acceptable with crops and can form useful shelter for animals.

27.4 Where a viaduct passes over water such as lakes, watermeadows, old gravel workings, flooded clay pits, etc., particularly where they are artificial, the opportunity can be taken to extend it under and around the structure. This avoids ugly areas of mud or paving beneath and enhances the structure's appearance by reflection and by improvement of its setting. This can be particularly appropriate under low broad structures, which otherwise might cause ecologically dead areas. The opportunity should be taken to encourage leisure facilities like active water sports – water-skiing, power boats, jet skis – which are appropriate to close proximity with roads. Balancing ponds can be utilized to give landscape features under viaducts and flyovers, although they should be low-maintenance; fountains should generally be avoided unless special maintenance arrangements are possible.

27.5 In urban areas it can be appropriate to have leisure or commercial uses under bridges and viaducts, as long as they do not interfere with structural maintenance. Areas of unusable hard paved landscape can be unpleasant if not carefully handled by the landscape architect, although the feeling of height and space can be very welcome. Sculpture and artist-designed paving can be appropriate (see Chapter 23) but must be used as an integral part of the landscape, in which signs and lighting are also integrated (see Chapter 22). Urban hard civic landscaping adjacent to the structure should be continued underneath where appropriate.

27.6 Sports facilities like hard football pitches, tennis courts, skateboard tracks, cricket nets, volleyball courts, running tracks, etc., can be accommodated, especially when associated with schools or sports centres. Open commercial leisure uses such as go-karting, miniature golf, pubs and restaurants or their terraces can also be appropriate, as can car parking. Buildings under structures can be appropriate, in urban areas, but should not prevent access to the structure for

27.3a (below) Usk Bridge, Abergavenny, Gwent. Shelter for cattle is a common and valid use.

27.4a (above) M3, Thorpe, Surrey. Active water sports are appropriate near noisy roads.

27.5a (right) Artist-designed Paving, Leith, Edinburgh: excellent scale of detail.

maintenance. Maintenance buildings and control rooms are good uses, as are markets and other such temporary buildings. There have been bus stations, youth clubs, cinemas and museums successfully located under road structures. The example of rail structures can be emulated. It is particularly important to have appropriate functions for landward spans of river bridges in cities.

27.6a (left) DELFT, Holland: car parking under flyover.

27.7 Anything which would encourage rubbish, fires and vagrants should be avoided.

27.6b (right) PORTOBELLO ROAD/WESTWAY, London: market under elevated road.

27.6d (below) WESTBOURNE PARK/WESTWAY, London: public transport depot integrated with elevated road.

27.6c (above) WATERLOO BRIDGE, South Bank, London: cinemas, museum, restaurant and market under bridge.

27.7a (right) WATERLOO BRIDGE, London: 'cardboard city' vagrant camp, threatening to both pedestrians and structures.

27.11a (above, left) M40 BRIDGE: planting zone under end-spans.

27.12a (above) M3, Thorpe, Surrey: unnecessary paving under end-span. Both light and rainwater can penetrate under the skew bridge.

27.15a (far left) CONCRETE PERFORATED BLOCKS, Autostrada del Sol, Italy.

27.15b (left) GREEN PLASTIC PAVERS.

27.8 When restoring old bridges, it may be important to retain existing uses of the space beneath, particularly boat stores, which enhance the appearance of the bridge and may be of historical interest.

27.9 Where there is insufficient light or rainfall, planting to match the adjacent landscape is not possible and alternative finishes are necessary. Where bridges are narrow and/or high, soft landscape will generally spread underneath. Lack of water tends to be more critical than lack of light, so plants will grow better under a viaduct over boggy ground, for instance. Special grass seed mixtures and plant varieties are available for areas under bridges. Beneath end-spans over fast roads, even the green of weeds can look better than hard paving since it is seen fleetingly.

27.10 The area where plants tend not to grow can roughly be defined by lines drawn on the cross-section of the bridge at 45° inwards from the bottom arris of the bridge deck cantilever, or similar position, or from any point on the section (e.g. a beam) which projects beyond that initial line. This will define a triangular or trapezoidal zone on the abutment slope and sometimes a band under the bridge, depending on its breadth and height. When the bridge is skewed, rain and light can penetrate to a surprising extent. The cut-off line is not sharply defined, having a very broad penumbra, so there is much scope for a change of finish at different positions, depending on local conditions.

27.11 Common and successful cut-off lines on abutment embankments when planting cannot continue fully under the bridge are:
● follow the line to give a triangle
● approximate the triangle but make it symmetrical for skew bridges
● take a line straight down the slope from the edge of the first beam where the edge cantilever starts.

27.12 Paving the full width under a bridge is unnecessary and looks heavy and crude. It can also appear to be part of the structure, especially where it joins a leaf pier to the abutment, causing visual confusion.

27.13 Finishes in the defined zone should be determined by the landscape architect to relate to the adjacent landscaping, and the bridge's specific and local context.

27.14 *Finishes and materials which have proved suitable fall into three categories: planted pavers, natural hard materials and artificial hard materials.*

27.15 Planted pavers are generally perforated plastic or concrete blocks or grids through which plants will grow. They provide a stable surface for access and pleasant textured patterns, which merge gradually into the grass or other planting. Concrete blocks give about 25% and plastic grids 75% planting area. Plastic may be coloured green, which

27.18a (right) M42, Solihull, West Midlands. Patterned paving such as chequerboard is not appropriate.

27.17a (below) M1/J1, North London: blockwork with cast in rocks.

can help give the impression of greenness flowing under the bridge, but black disappears better. Both can take emergency vehicular loads. Concrete, therefore, may be better for large areas, while plastic may tend to visually eliminate small areas.

27.16 Natural hard materials include brick paving, stone slabs, stone setts, set cobbles, gravel, rock scree, flints, boulders, rocks set to echo local natural rock formations, loose pebbles, bark mulch, wood chips and recycled wood block paving. All these have a good appearance and should be used in preference to artificial materials where possible. Some, especially those which are loose, may not be appropriate in all situations. Many other materials have potential for use.

27.17 Artificial hard materials are generally less satisfactory than natural materials and planted pavers but have a useful role, especially where loose materials might be a liability for vandalism and access reasons. Proprietary concrete

blocks incorporating rough rocks, concrete anti-pedestrian paving, plain and textured concrete paving slabs of various shapes, in situ concrete with exposed aggregate finish, and tarmac with a gravel top dressing, can be suitable.

27.18 Ornamental patterns such as chequerboards or more exotic designs should be avoided generally, since the intention is to draw one's attention away from such areas. The exception would be when the finish forms part of a larger paving design for the whole area in urban schemes. The landscape should flow through and the bridge read as a complete structure in itself.

PICTURE CREDITS
27.3a ph JW. **27.4a** ph JW. **27.5a** ph JW. **27.6a** ph JW. **27.6b d** Ted Happold; ph JW. **27.6c** ph JW. **27.6d d** GLC; ph JW. **27.7a** ph JW. **27.11a d** Arup. **27.15a** ph JW. **27.15b d** Bartron Corporation. **27.17a** ph JW. **27.18a** ph JW.

Chapter 28
Ancillary buildings

28.1 *A choice must always be made between relating the appearance of ancillary buildings either to the local environment or to the road.* The architect should carry out an appraisal and provide justification for the choice.

28.2 All ancillary buildings should be designed by a registered architect, and the highest design quality sought. The design should be appropriate to its location, but where a vernacular or even a classical design is appropriate, this should not degenerate into pastiche; an architect known for working within the appropriate approach should be appointed.

28.3 Service buildings to tunnels, especially incorporating vent shafts, tend to be in environmentally sensitive

28.1a (above) SERVICE BUILDING, Conway Tunnel, Gwynedd: insensitive design relating to road.

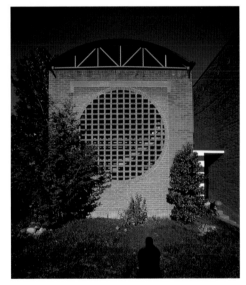

28.2a (right) CASA OSTINELLI, Vacallo, Switzerland: contemporary architecture with appropriate scale and quality of detail.

28.1b (left) SERVICE BUILDING, Pen y Clip Tunnel, North Wales: sensitive vernacular design relating to environment.

28.2c (right) LIBRARY ANNEXE, Cambridge: appropriate insular secure store.

28.2b (above) PUBLIC TOILETS, Notting Hill, London: a striking modern example.

28.4a (below) UNDERGROUND
SERVICE BUILDING, A27,
Salvington Tunnel, West Sussex.

28.4b (right) TUNNEL VENT,
Victoria Line, Islington, London:
exquisite classical design for a
formal square.

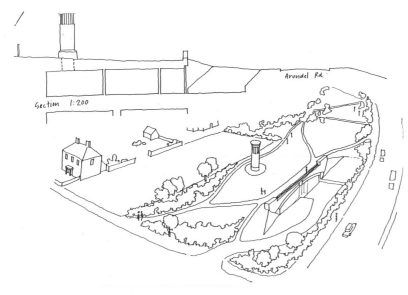

28.4c (above, left) UNDERGROUND
SERVICE BUILDING, Ferreira,
Portugal.

28.4d (above) UNDERGROUND
SERVICE BUILDING, Ronchamp,
France.

28.4e (left) LIMEHOUSE LINK,
Docklands, London: underground
services building.

locations, and whilst easy access by road and to the road within the tunnel is necessary, they need not be near the road. The open yard and secure compound fence are often the most difficult items to accommodate in a pleasant way. A building surrounding a courtyard is often a satisfactory solution and is appropriate to both a vernacular and a contemporary solution.

28.4 In rural areas with no buildings locally, a buried solution can be appropriate. In rural areas with occasional buildings, either dwellings or farm buildings, designs in the local vernacular can be appropriate, but a 'Disneyland' pastiche should be avoided. In formal landscape areas a design inspired by formal garden buildings or follies can be appropriate, especially where the site has to be prominent. Visually functional vents can also be appropriate.

28.5a (above) Vent Shaft, Centre Pompidou, Paris: *trompe l'oeil* vent shaft to repair townscape.

28.5b (above, right) Service Building, Limehouse Link, Docklands, London: exciting contemporary architecture (?) at Canary Wharf.

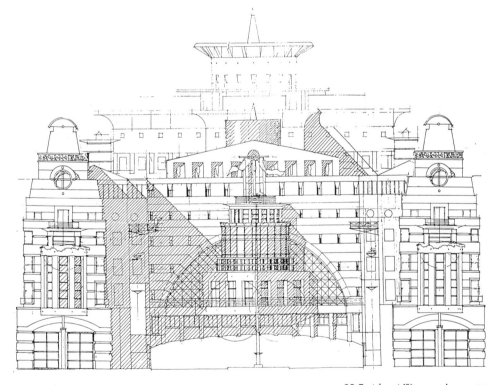

28.5d (below) Service Building, Unité, Marseilles, France.

28.5c (above) Western Approach Road, Edinburgh: civic development incorporating road tunnel.

28.5 In urban locations the building should be appropriate in form and materials to the townscape, and where possible fill vacant sites caused by the new road. In regenerating areas the opportunity can be taken to encourage exciting contemporary architecture around a new tunnel (see Chapter 17).

28.6 In rest areas, whether they be full-scale motorway service facilities, small laybys or the equivalent of the French Aires de Repos with toilets, picnic areas and extensive landscaped parking with view points, the site and landscaping are all-important. Since their purpose is for road users to rest, the buildings and landscape should be relaxing and tranquil, using water, natural materials and soft landscaping, and preferably separated from the road by natural topographical features or existing mature woodland. Distant and/or beautiful views from the site should be exploited and enhanced. Sites within woodland are best. Beautiful buildings and landscape help relaxation.

28.7 Wherever possible, existing historic buildings should be used for rest area buildings. Where the proximity of a road renders them less appropriate for their current use, their potential as part of a rest area should be exploited to promote such use of the site, as opposed to any green field site.

28.6a (above) AIRE DE REPOS, Limoges, France.

28.6b (above, right) AIRE DE REPOS, A40, Chamonix.

28.6c (right) TEBAY WEST, Cumbria: tranquil view from service area.

28.6d (above, centre) PICNIC AREA, A320, Staines, Surrey: idyllic design.

28.7a (left) M40, Warwick: suitable old buildings for a service area.

28.7b (above) L'AIRE DE CAISSARGNES, A54, near Nîmes, France: reused historic façade set off well with formal landscaping.

28.8a (below) SERVICE BUILDINGS, Tebay, Cumbria. They relate well to the location.

28.8b (below) AIRE DU COMBARETTES, A8, France: a simple building in the local vernacular for the public conveniences.

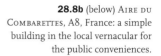

28.8c (above) VILLAGE CATALAN, A9, Perpignan, France. This pastiche vernacular village for a motorway service area is well executed, but genuine old buildings would have been better.

28.9a (above) MOTORWAY SERVICE AREA, A11, Parcé-sur-Sarthe, France. Obvious entrance and routes to building are enhanced by formal landscaping.

28.9b (right) L'AIRE DE MANOSQUE, A51, Manosque, France. Simple access routes, woodland and water humanize this motorway-scale building.

28.8 The design of buildings should relate to the locality to help drivers' orientation along their journey. Ideally, so should the interior design (and food). Standardized buildings are inappropriate in most situations, especially for motels, unless an architect uses a flexible kit of parts to make the form, finishes, plan layout, materials and roof design of the building appropriate to its setting.

28.9 Restaurant and motel buildings should be welcoming, with obvious entrances, a human scale and the entrance well lit at night. The vehicle and pedestrian routes should be simple and clear, especially at night.

28.10a (above) FLOODLIT SIGNBOARD: unnecessary light pollution.

28.12a (left) TOLL PLAZA, A83, Bignon, France: a simple, elegant design.

28.12b (right) TOLL PLAZA, Lançon, A7, Provence, France: perhaps too baroque and monumental for its function.

28.14a (right) BORDER CROSSING, Le Perthus, Spain/France: monument to Catalunya, using spoil from road construction.

28.10 Light pollution, particularly from parking areas and signs, is a common problem. Full cut-off lighting should be used with no upward directed floodlights, and no low-pressure sodium lamps because of their orange glow and lack of ability to be focused.

28.11 Toll plazas and border controls tend to be large, open, brightly lit and obtrusive. Topographically hidden sites are best, and these can be anywhere along the length of tolled road, not necessarily at the start or end. One-way tolling on bridges is preferable since a toll plaza at the other end is not needed.

28.12 Toll plazas usually should relate to the road. They should be fine examples of contemporary architecture and express and celebrate their function. Associated buildings such as toilets, staff offices and retail facilities should be part of the overall design.

28.13 Light pollution should again be avoided.

28.14 Bold landscape or architectural features can occasionally be appropriate to draw the attention away from unsightly features, especially where there is a suitable symbolic purpose such as a national border.

28.15 *Control buildings to opening bridges* also should usually relate to the road environment and be prominent and distinctive, since road and waterway users need to see the control room. Large viewing windows, shelter for pedestrians and space for noticeboards (for opening times, tide tables, operating instructions, etc.) should be integrated into the design (see Chapter 15).

PICTURE CREDITS
28.1a ph JW. **28.1b d** Travers Morgan; ph JW. **28.2a d** Ivano Gianola. **28.2b d** Piers Gough. **28.2c** ph JW. **28.4a d** Acer. **28.4b d** Quinlan Terry; ph JW. **28.4c** ph JW. **28.4d d** Le Corbusier; ph JW. **28.4e d** Anthony Meats; ph JW. **28.5a d** Richard Rogers/Renzo Piano; ph JW. **28.5b d** Anthony Meats; ph JW. **28.5c d** Terry Farrell. **28.5d d** Le Corbusier; ph JW. **28.6a** ph JW. **28.6b** ph JW. **28.6c** ph JW. **28.6d** ph JW. **28.7a** ph JW. **28.7b d** Bernard Lassus. **28.8a** ph JW. **28.8b** ph Jerome Chatin. **28.8c d** Bertran de Balanda. **28.9a** ph Alain Szczuczynski. **28.9b** ph Jerome Chatin. **28.10a** ph IDA/APS. **28.12a d** Beguin and Macchini; ph Yannick Collet. **28.12b d** Henry Focillon. **28.14a d** Ricardo Bofill; ph JW.

Chapter 29

Retaining walls

29.1 Retaining walls can be:

- part of the approach to a tunnel
- associated with bridges over cuttings
- retaining cuttings with no associated bridge structure
- retaining a road on embankment usually associated with a bridge structure.

Many of the comments are common to all situations, though some relate only to specific situations or forms of construction.

29.2 *Retaining walls are best minimized in size and extent. This can be done both physically and visually.*

29.3 Before detailing the wall, check whether its size can be reduced by fine tuning of the road level and alignment, e.g. by having carriageways at different levels, or putting footpaths further from the road at different levels.

29.4 Where an environmental barrier or pedestrian guardrail is required at the top of a retaining wall, it is rarely a good solution to continue the latter visually to incorporate the barrier or rail. It is better to separate the elements and place the environmental barrier or rail back from the retaining wall and possibly on a different alignment related to the environment beyond the new road. Planting between the two structures helps to soften and reduce the size and impact of both, but any barriers for maintenance staff for such planting need to be considered and integrated if the drop is over 1.5m.

29.5 Where a retaining wall can be set back from the road, or is required for sightlines, a planted embankment should be located at the foot of the wall. This reduces the apparent height and softens the appearance. Likewise, where the retaining wall can be built in a series of steps, planting can soften the appearance at multiple levels; as well as each wall being smaller, they tend to be hidden by perspective.

29.6 The end of a retaining wall can be curved in plan to return into the hillside, and to form a planted embankment in front of this end to emphasize the effect. This can considerably reduce the length of the low ends of retaining walls.

29.7 Retaining walls have their greatest impact when new, before planting has grown and local people have become used to their presence. Any opportunity should be taken to plant very large mature trees – perhaps 10m high – in front of such walls, as part of the landscaping scheme. They need large volumes of uncompacted soil, particularly when first planted, but this can be achieved by early collaboration between the engineer and landscape architect. Fast-growing climbing plants may also be considered, which need a smaller planting pit, but may need to be on a removable trellis to facilitate inspection of the structure.

29.8 When near a carriageway, a smooth surface is often required for approximately the bottom 1.2m of a retaining wall for safety reasons. This can be exploited since this plinth can visually form a part of the road if detailed correctly, thus reducing the apparent height of the retaining wall. To achieve this, it is important to make the finish relate to the road and to any immediately adjacent hard strip of paving. Also the height, shape and plane of the plinth should match and run into any adjacent low retaining structure or vertical concrete barrier (VCB). This approach can be particularly successful where the finish of the main part of the wall contrasts with the plinth, e.g. is clad with stone or brick.

29.9 The pattern of the wall finish can have an apparent visual effect on the size of the wall. Horizontal patterns reduce height but emphasize length, whilst vertical patterns can emphasize the height. A visually heavy coping obviates these positive effects by emphasizing the actual height.

29.4a (above) SADDLEWORTH, Greater Manchester: walls separated with planting between.

29.9a (above) VELASQUEZ BRIDGE CUTTING, Toulouse, France. Pattern visually reduces height.

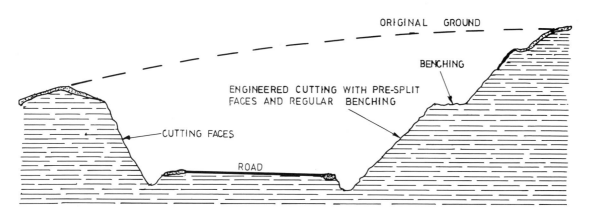

ORIGINAL GROUND

BENCHING

ENGINEERED CUTTING WITH PRE-SPLIT
FACES AND REGULAR BENCHING

CUTTING FACES

ROAD

29.12a (left)
ROCK FACES:
harsh treatment,
only rarely
preferable.

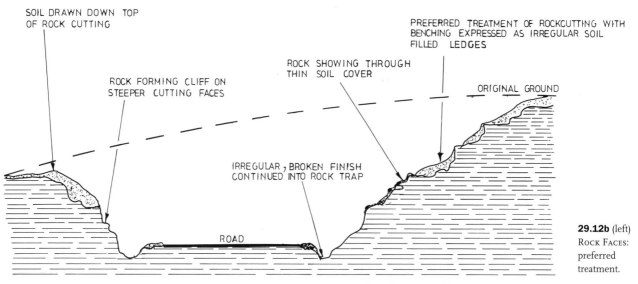

SOIL DRAWN DOWN TOP
OF ROCK CUTTING

ROCK FORMING CLIFF ON
STEEPER CUTTING FACES

ROCK SHOWING THROUGH
THIN SOIL COVER

PREFERRED TREATMENT OF ROCKCUTTING WITH
BENCHING EXPRESSED AS IRREGULAR SOIL
FILLED LEDGES

ORIGINAL GROUND

IRREGULAR, BROKEN FINISH
CONTINUED INTO ROCK TRAP

ROAD

29.12b (left)
ROCK FACES:
preferred
treatment.

29.10 See *The Good Roads Guide* (Design Manual for Roads and Bridges, Volume 10, Section 1, Part 4, Chapter 3) for further landscaping techniques to minimize the impact of retaining walls.

29.11 *Context should usually have a strong influence on choice of materials.* With retaining walls the usual preference for honesty, expressing structure and avoiding cladding, sometimes need not take precedence since it often does not lead to a beautiful solution. To think of a retaining wall in the same way as the façade of a building may help understanding of the quantity and quality of visual detail necessary to produce a suitable appearance in its context. However, this is usually best derived from carefully thought out geometry and a structural system which is inherently visually suitable, and derives its expression from its structural reality.

29.12 *The best solutions to retaining the ground are natural ones: rock cliffs and planted embankments.* These should always be pursued where possible, even if only for one of a series of retaining walls or only part of a very large wall. Observational methods should be used to maximize the steepness of specific parts of each site, and to remove or restrain parts of the surface. In most cases a careful naturalistic treatment of cut rock faces is preferable, though the drama of a sharp, sheer rock cut can sometimes be exploited.

29.13a (above) A27 BRIGHTON
BYPASS: textile reinforced slope
before grass has grown, showing
steepness possible.

29.13 Where the rock or earth slope cannot stand by itself, concealed aids should be considered, e.g. nailing, rock anchors, geotextile fabric-reinforced slopes or hydroseeding of special plants. Advances in techniques of bio-engineering increase the opportunity for using 'soft' solutions.

29.14 Where concealed support is not possible, the ground should be supported by simple visible aids such as masonry or concrete buttresses or buttress arches, gabions, armour stone blocks, visible rock anchors, dark-coloured rock netting, stone walling to strengthen weak parts of cliffs, or dark-coloured rock fences. Bridge abutments and the structural action of the bridge itself can be used to strengthen weak natural slopes in cuttings, especially since the bridge itself is often logically where there is maximum height of retention.

29.15 Where some form of structure proves necessary, the simplest and most natural form is usually best, in particular where the height to be retained is small or where it can be made to be small by using steps (see Paragraph 29.5).

29.14a (left) MASONRY BUTTRESSES, Ticino, Switzerland: good attention to rustic detail.

29.14b (below) GABIONS, Penmaen-Bach, North Wales: a useful technique, improved by broken geometry.

29.14c (below) ROCK ANCHORS, Pen y Clip, North Wales: a simple, unpretentious engineering solution.

29.14d (right) ROCK FENCE ON SCREE, Pen y Clip, North Wales. The fence disappears; when this photograph was taken the concrete blocks had not yet been painted dark.

29.16 Where there are traditional walling techniques in the area appropriate for low retaining structures, these should be used, e.g. Cornish hedgebanks, Devon banks, dry stone walls, flint walls, or boundary walls to local estates or industrial complexes. It is very important to get the materials and details of construction exactly correct, since these can vary in a short distance due to local circumstances.

For example, round boulders are used in walling near rivers, but broken rocks further away, and changes in stone used can follow a change in geology, e.g. a fault line. An architect should be used to detail historic and urban masonry walls, though a landscape architect may be more appropriate to detail traditional rural walls and hedgebanks.

29.16a (far left) SOMPTING, West Sussex: flint wall giving inspiration for adjacent bypass boundary.

29.16b (left) BINGLEY BYPASS, West Yorkshire: stone wall to match adjacent factory.

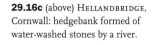
29.16c (above) HELLANDBRIDGE, Cornwall: hedgebank formed of water-washed stones by a river.

29.16d (above, right) HELLANDBRIDGE, Cornwall: rough stones and heavy planting at edge of village.

29.16e (right) HELLANDBRIDGE, Cornwall: roughly square stones at change of geology.

29.17a (right) M40, High Wycombe, Buckinghamshire: gabions for retaining cut on a successful road widening.

29.18a (below) Eastern Gateway Access Road, London Docklands: timber crib wall with good planting.

29.20a (below, right) Hampstead Hill, North London: log wall.

29.21a (bottom, right) Retaining Wall, near Calais, France: unusual, boldy expressed sheet piling.

29.17 Gabions are almost always an excellent solution. Their filling should be of stone appropriate to the local area. Loose filling is generally suitable, but coursed-laid stone can look very good if the local stone is appropriate. This is particularly suitable for motorway widening where planted cutting slopes can be retained. The height limit is 1.4m, and generally it cannot be used to retain the road itself.

29.18 Modular crib-wall systems in timber and concrete can be used, but it is very important to provide topsoil behind the structure to ensure that the planting can grow over it. The smaller scale and natural materials of timber systems are very much preferable to concrete, since they can look pleasant in their own right before planting develops. Concrete crib walls should only be used where planting is likely to be fast-growing and luxuriant.

29.19 Proprietary modular concrete or clay block retaining walls can look effective when the full scope of the system is utilized by the landscape architect, in particular by using steps and curves.

29.20 Timber log walls, driven timber posts and old railway sleepers look good for low retaining walls as part of a landscaping scheme, often in semi-urban areas.

29.21 Sheet pile retaining walls can have advantages of minimal disturbance to existing planting, and can look good if carefully detailed. They should be painted black or another dark colour to minimize impact. The capping and/or walings should be discrete. Marine-style timber balk capping is very much preferable to heavy in situ concrete capping. Steel walings should be behind the wall covered by soil, or used as a capping, where the thin edge of a steel angle is least obtrusive. Exposed sheet piles are suitable when seen mostly at speed, from a distance, or when associated with urban river

29.22a (right) Aspen Way, London Docklands. Reinforced earth wall panels totally fail to mask real joint by using shallow false joints.

29.22b (far left) Vauxhall Cross, London: false joints of the same width and depth as real joints.

29.22c (left) Bank Façade, San Francisco, California: repeated decorative pattern.

reclamation. In appropriate circumstances such as industrial estates or new towns the nature of sheet piling can be celebrated and exploited. It can also be clad where a better finish is required but its practical advantages are needed.

29.22 Proprietary reinforced earth systems using precast concrete panels, or occasionally steel or fabric sheets tied with metal or fabric straps through earth layers, are almost invariably hideous, though this is probably because of manufacturers' emphasis on cheapness rather than any inherent fault of the technique. The panel shape is fixed for technical reasons, but is frequently rectangular, hexagonal, T-shaped or Maltese cross-shaped. This repeated pattern is of a large scale and relates to the road not the environment, increasing the intrusion of the road. The plain panels should

only be used where appearance matters little; in all other situations panels should be specially cast to a location-specific design. The principle of any design should be to break down the scale and repetition of the modules. The emphasis of the joints between panels needs to be lost, usually by modelling and false joints which, to be effective, must be the same width and depth as the true joints to give the same depth of shadow. If the true joints penetrate the entire panel, the false should be at least as deep as the width of the joint to give adequate shadow depth. Patterns using vertical or horizontal banding and imitation dressed ashlar have proved successful. The use of natural colours using coloured aggregates or pigments has great potential. An alternative technique in certain circumstances is to celebrate the repetition by casting repeated sculptural images in every or alternate panels.

29.23 In situ concrete walls are often used and are very adaptable, but their brutalist appearance and their proneness to graffiti makes them unpopular and unsightly (see Chapter 20). They also tend to weather badly. Smooth finishes with or without the joints and fixings expressed are rarely suitable, especially where pedestrians will be close. They should be limited to areas of wall associated with road surfaces or bridges, e.g. the base of walls (see above). Textured surfaces can be obtained as described in Chapter 20, as well as by placing boulders in the formwork to give a wall similar to a rubble stone wall.

The repeated patterns of form liners are difficult to disguise when seen in perspective or from a distance. The use of an artist to produce a sculptured design either in the formwork, in a form liner, or direct into a fresh or full strength concrete was at one time popular, and still has potential, but it is best viewed in a soft, planted environment, e.g. a park (see also Chapters 20 and 23). It is difficult to relate any in situ concrete wall to the natural environment, and one should question whether an urban environment with existing in situ concrete surfaces is improved by further concrete walls, even if they are effectively the local vernacular.

29.24 *Many structural forms for retaining walls can be clad for appearance or acoustic reasons, and some, such as contiguous bored piles, require it.* Cladding methods can be divided into (a) masonry (b) large panel (c) noise attenuating. *All such clad walls require a large visual design input and are often decorative.* Usually in rural areas and almost always in urban areas they will require an architect to design and detail them.

29.25 Water seepage through all types of cladding can be an unsightly problem, and suitable drainage with overflows and accessibility for cleaning is always important.

29.26 Masonry cladding is generally in stone, brick or concrete blockwork, and the detailing and possible patterning depend on the particular material and the coursing. This can either be horizontal or follow the profile of the surface at the base of the wall. For practical reasons it cannot follow the profile of the top of the wall.

29.23a (below, left) WATERLOO UNDERPASS, London. In situ smooth concrete attracts graffiti.

29.23c (below) TALIESIN WEST, Phoenix, Arizona, USA: boulders in the formwork.

29.26a (above) INNER RING ROAD, Coventry: an elegant, simple, brick-clad retaining wall with strong colour and planting.

29.23b (left) PEN Y CLIP, North Wales: stepped sawn-board wall.

29.27a (top) BRIDSTOW BRIDGE, Ross-on-Wye: uncoursed masonry.

29.30a (above) ISOLA BELLA, Lake Maggiore, Italy: baroque retaining wall.

29.29a (top, right) AVENUE DE CHARTRES, Chichester, West Sussex. Horizontal coursing makes a diagonal pattern possible.

29.30b (right) DECORATIVE ARCH FORMS.

29.27 Following the road profile avoids awkward cutting at the base and the need to mask it by a nib at the base, which can avoid problems with drainage. Since the perpends are not vertical, no vertical lines can be expressed, whether for patterns, buttresses or expansion joints. It can therefore only be used for simple plain walls, and is well suited to blockwork. Banded patterns following the coursing in contrasting colours or textures of the same material or in different materials, like blockwork with bands of coloured glazed brick, can be a successful way of using patterns to break up the surface of large walls. Rubble stonework is best uncoursed, which can then follow the road profile. If it is coursed and follows the road profile, it will tend to return to horizontal further up the wall, so should start horizontal if the local traditional detail is for coursed rubble walling.

29.28 Projecting string-courses are a useful device for changing coursing. This may be from following the road profile to horizontal coursing or to it following a parapet which may itself be following an upper road on the far side of the wall on a different profile. The same device is useful on stone and brick bridges. Such functional features should be the starting point for any elaboration of detail necessary for its location (see Chapter 23).

29.29 Horizontal coursing allows much more scope for elaborate design. Ashlar stone walling must be horizontal for practical reasons, and brick should generally be horizontally coursed unless it is very plain. The surface of of brick and stone cladding can be modelled or patterned with colour or texture, or both.

29.30 Modelling is usually based on the appearance of traditional loadbearing masonry walls since it visually expresses its function of a retaining wall and can have a certain genuine structural function of partially supporting itself. Suitable forms are battering, piers, arches, inverted arches, arcades and recessed panels. The deeper and bolder the modelling, the better it generally appears, and also the more realistic as a retaining wall. The enormous variety of possible arch shapes should be exploited, and local examples can form useful inspiration. The boldness of Victorian brickwork and the exuberant detail of baroque forms can give suitably large scale for road schemes.

29.31 Pattern is particularly suitable for brick, although patterns such as Anglo-Saxon long and short work, garneted joints in chalk, flint and stone chequerboard, contrasted rough and smooth stone, and alternating colours of voussoirs have potential for stone. The vast palette of Victorian decorative brick patterns should not be ignored since they derive from the nature of the material and may be appropriate in certain situations; but it is best to use the nature of the material to produce new ideas of patterns and form, such as images – people or trees – or patterns like those derived from geology or Jacquard weaving. Ceramic tiles can also be used to face retaining walls in pedestrian locations, and pattern is then very important (see Chapters 16 and 23).

29.32 Brick or (artificial) stone specials can be used with both modelling and pattern to give further possibilities such as quoins, keystone, voussoirs, string-courses, capitals, copings, pier caps, gargoyles, etc., as part of traditional or modern designs. Brick specials should be kept as simple and geometric as possible, but cast stone can be highly modelled and sculpted with negligible additional cost.

29.33 On large-size precast concrete panels the wide range of colour and texture possible with different aggregates, cements, pigments and surface treatments such as retarders, acid-washing, sandblasting and polishing should be exploited. Applying finishes to precast panels such as brickwork, tiles and loose aggregate either before or after casting has proved less visually satisfactory and often weathers badly or fails to bond permanently. The treatment of panel joints is critical, especially where the large scale of the system needs to be

29.33a (right) PEN Y CLIP, North Wales: rock anchor panels in knocked-off rib pattern.

29.31a (below) VELASQUEZ BRIDGE, Toulouse, France: pattern created by marble, precast concrete and rock anchors.

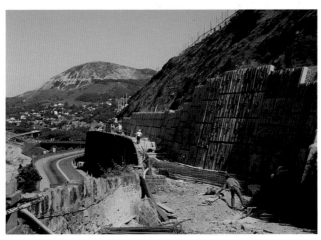

29.33b (above) PEN Y CLIP, North Wales: rock anchor panels in cast patterns.

29.33c (above) THAMES RIVER WALL, Vauxhall: precast cladding to sheet piling.

29.34a (left) Velasquez bridge, Toulouse: terracotta noise-absorbent panels.

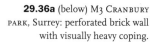

29.36a (below) M3 Cranbury park, Surrey: perforated brick wall with visually heavy coping.

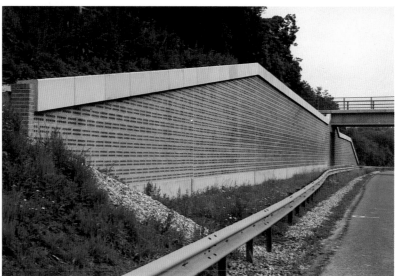

reduced visually. Any false joints should match the real joints in width and depth. Joints can be lost visually by putting joints in returns or by overlapping panels and pilasters or string-courses. Sculpture can be easily incorporated where appropriate, cast from rubber moulds. Bold modelling is usually best and works particularly well when exploiting functional features such as drain overflows, doors, access panels, lamp fixings, etc. Large flat surfaces are best avoided, especially where seen by pedestrians, and modelled patterns are easily incorporated. In underpasses or other areas where surfaces are likely to get very dirty, bold modelling is particularly important.

29.34 Noise-attenuating cladding is increasingly used, especially in urban areas (see also Chapter 24). In principle, a surface with a large number of pores or voids and/or a soft flexible material is required to dissipate the energy of the noise-laden air. Many manufacturers are now developing suitable materials, but the skills of a specialist architect are vital to achieve a satisfactory result.

29.35 In principle, the noise-absorbing surface can be anywhere in the road environment, i.e. not necessarily between the vehicle and the listener, so the road surface (porous asphalt) and the central reservation (barrier or road surface) are suitable locations for noise absorbency, as well as retaining walls.

Because tunnels are perfect at removing noise from the adjacent environment, the contrast between the noise at the approaches and in the tunnel itself makes the approach appear worse than any other part of the road, although it may be actually no more severe. The retaining walls at tunnel approaches, especially in urban areas, therefore often may need noise attenuation (see Chapter 17).

29.36 Absorbent walls usually have a perforated weathering skin on the surface and voids beyond, often lined with an acoustically absorbent material. The skin can be perforated bricks on edge, perforated blocks (either proprietary or standard designs), brickwork, blockwork or stonework laid with open joints or larger voids, perforated sheet metal or fibre cement sheets, perforated precast concrete panels or timber cladding. The absorbent material in the void can usually not be seen, so its visual characteristics are not important. However, it should be able to withstand the weathering conditions relative to its exposure, be vandal-resistant as necessary and not vulnerable to attack or nesting by birds or insects, all of which would otherwise have long-term effects on appearance. Proprietary products combining the skin and absorbent material are being developed. Care must be taken to avoid visual confusion between environmental barriers, clad retaining walls and tunnel linings, especially where lightweight claddings are used. (For the design of environmental barriers refer to HA65/94, DMRB, Volume 10, Section 5, Part 1.)

Picture Credits
29.4a ph JW. **29.9a d** Alain Spielmann; ph JW. **29.12a d** Richard Moorehead and Laing. **29.12b d** Richard Moorehead and Laing. **29.13a** ph JW. **29.14a** ph JW. **29.14b d** Travers Morgan; ph JW. **29.14c d** Travers Morgan; ph JW. **29.14d d** Travers Morgan; ph JW. **29.16a** ph JW. **29.16b** ph JW. **29.16c** ph JW. **29.16d** ph JW. **29.16e** ph JW. **29.17a** ph JW. **29.18a** ph JW. **29.20a** ph JW. **29.21a** ph British Steel. **29.22a** ph JW. **29.22b d** Terry Farrell; ph JW. **29.23a d** Nicholas Grimshaw. **29.23b d** Travers Morgan; ph JW. **29.23c d** Frank Lloyd Wright; ph JW. **29.26a** ph JW. **29.27a** ph JW. **29.29a d** Birds Portchmouth Russum; ph JW. **29.30b** From *Historical Architectural Plans, Details and Elements*, John Haneman. **29.31a d** Alain Spielmann; ph JW. **29.33a d** Travers Morgan; ph JW. **29.33b d** Travers Morgan; ph JW. **29.33c d** Terry Farrell; ph JW. **29.34a d** Alain Spielmann; ph JW.

Bibliography

GENERAL

BROWN, David J. *Bridges: Three Thousand Years of Defying Nature*. Mitchell Beazley, 1993. ISBN 1-85732-163-4.

CERVER, Francisco Asensio, ed. *New Architecture, Puentes/Bridges*. Atrium, 1992. ISBN 84-7741-175-1,

CULLEN, Gordon. *Townscape*. Architectural Press, 1961.

DELONY, Eric. *Landmark American Bridges*. American Society of Civil Engineers, 1992. ISBN 0-87262-857-4.

DE MARÉ, Eric. *Bridges of Britain*. Revised Edition. Batsford, 1975.

FIELDHOUSE, Kenneth, ed. *Landscape Design*, bridges special issue. Landscape Institute, November 1992. ISSN 0020-2908.

HOULET, Jacques. *Éléments pour une Théorie du Paysage Autoroutier*. Autoroutes du Sud de la France, 1993.

INGLIS, CE, ed. *The Aesthetic Aspect of Civil Engineering Design*. Institution of Civil Engineers, 1944.

JACKSON, Donald C. *Great American Bridges and Dams*. The Preservation Press, 1988. ISBN 0-89133-129-8.

LEONHARDT, Fritz. *Brücken/Bridges*. Architectural Press, 1982. ISBN 0-85139-764-6.

MAINSTONE, Rowland J. *Developments in Structural Form*. Allen/Royal Institute of British Architects, 1975. ISBN 0-7139-0333-3.

MARYLAND DEPARTMENT OF TRANSPORTATION. *Aesthetic Bridges, Users' Guide*. Maryland State Highway Administration, 1995.

NORWEGIAN STATE HIGHWAYS DEPARTMENT. *Utforming av bruer*. Vegdirektoratet Handboksekretariatet, 1992. ISBN 82-7207-321-8.

PLOWDEN, David. *Bridges: The Spans of North America*. WW Norton & Co., 1974. ISBN 0-393-01936-5.

ROYAL FINE ART COMMISSION. *Bridge Design: the RFAC Seminar*. HMSO, 1993. ISBN 0-11-752793-9.

RUDDOCK, Ted. *Arch Bridges and their Builders 1735–1835*. Cambridge University Press, 1979.

THE SCOTTISH OFFICE. *Roads, Bridges and Traffic in the Countryside*. SOID Roads Directorate, 1992. ISBN 0-748005-86-2.

STEINMAN, David B. and WATSON, Sara S. *Bridges and their Builders*. GP Putnam Sons, 1941.

TORRES, Antonio Alles, ed. *Puentes 1, 2, & 3*. Colegio de Ingenieros de Caminos, Canales y Puertos, Barcelona, 1991. ISSN 0213-4195.

TRANSPORTATION RESEARCH BOARD. Committee on General Structures: Subcommittee on Bridge Aesthetics. *Bridge Aesthetics Around the World*. United States National Research Council, 1991. ISSN 0360-859-x.

DETAILED

Chapter 1

CANTACUZINO, Sherban. *What Makes a Good Building?* Royal Fine Art Commission, 1994. ISBN 0-9523321-08.

HILLMANN, Judy. *Planning for Beauty*. RFAC/HMSO, 1990. ISBN 0-11-752275-9.

Chapter 2

DEPARTMENT OF TRANSPORT. *Good Roads Guide*. HMSO, 1992.

McCLUSKEY, J. *Road Form and Townscape*. Architectural Press, 1979. ISBN 0-85139-548-1.

Chapter 3

BUTLER, ASG. *The Architecture of Sir Edwin Lutyens*. Volume 2. Country Life, 1950.

Chapter 4

BILL, Max. *Robert Maillart: Bridges and Constructions*. Third Edition. Pall Mall Press, 1969.

BILLINGTON, David P. *Robert Maillart and the Art of Reinforced Concrete*. MIT Press, 1989. ISBN 0-262-02310-5.

MENN, Christian. *Prestressed Concrete Bridges*. Birkhauser, 1992. ISBN 0-8176-2414-7.

Chapter 6

CARDIFF UNIVERSITY SCHOOL OF ENGINEERING. Unpublished research.

Chapter 9

PODOLNY, Walter Jr and SCAIZI, John B. *Construction and Design of Cable-stayed Bridges*. Second Edition. John Wiley, 1986. ISBN 0-471-82655-3.

TROITSKY, MS. *Cable-stayed Bridges: Theory and Design*. Second Edition. BSP Professional Books, 1988. ISBN 0-632-02041-5.

Chapter 12

REIACH HALL BLYTH PARTNERSHIP. *Footbridges in the Countryside*. Country Commission for Scotland, 1981. ISBN 1-85397-040-9.

Chapter 16

STROM, Marianne. *Métro-Art dans les Métro-poles*. Jacques Damase Editeur, 1990. ISBN 2-904632-29-8.

Chapter 20

CEMENT & CONCRETE ASSOCIATION. *The Appearance of Concrete Highway Structures*. C&CA, 1972. ISBN 0-7210-1071-7.

GAGE, Michael. *Guide to Exposed Concrete Finishes*. Architectural Press, 1970. ISBN 0-85139-262-8.

HAWES, Frank. *The Weathering of Concrete Buildings*. C&CA, 1986. ISBN 0-7210-1333-3.

SWEDISH CORROSION INSTITUTE. *Weathering Steels in Building*. Swedish Council for Building Research, 1985. ISBN 91-540-4457-x.

TILLER, RM and WARD, FW. *Concrete Finishes for Highway Structures*. C&CA, 1972. ISBN 0-7210-0735-x.

Chapter 21

VARLEY, Helen, ed. *Colour*. Mitchell Beazley, 1980. ISBN 0-86134-024-8.

Chapter 22

DEPARTMENT OF TRANSPORT. *Road Lighting and the Environment*. DoT NMDI, 1993.

Chapter 24

HIGHWAYS AGENCY. *Design Guide for Environmental Barriers. HA 65/94*. HMSO, 1994.

Chapter 25

CARTWRIGHT, Richard D. *The Design of Urban Space*. Architectural Press, 1980. ISBN 0-85139-694-1.

Chapter 26

GIES, Joseph. *Bridges and Men*. Cassell, 1964.

TORRES, Antonio Alles, ed. *Revista OP, Puentes 1*. Colegio de Ingenieros de Caminos, Canales y Puertos, Barcelona, 1991. ISSN 0213-4195.

Chapter 28

HRH THE PRINCE OF WALES. *A Vision of Britain*. Doubleday, 1989. ISBN 0-385-6903-x.

The Appearance of Bridges and Other Highway Structures

Printed in the United Kingdom for The Stationery Office Ltd
Dd 0302323 C50 10/96 59226